DISORDERLY
CONDUCT

The Oddities Of My 20-Year Life As An FBI Special Agent

John Iannarelli

INDIE BOOKS
INTERNATIONAL®

ISBN-13: 978-1-952233-49-4
Library of Congress Control Number: 2021903030

Designed by Joni McPherson

INDIE BOOKS INTERNATIONAL, INC.˙
2424 VISTA WAY, SUITE 316
OCEANSIDE, CA 92054
www.indiebooksintl.com

For Garrett and Samantha.

For those in law enforcement, especially the FBI.

CONTENTS

Introduction

O ver the years, much has been written about the FBI. There are all sorts of books that tell the stories of great cases, great agents, and the Bureau's great history. From gun battles to organized crime, political corruption and, of course, terrorism, the FBI has been everywhere, involved in everything. All of these things have been written in one place or another and are readily available to the reader motivated to learn about them.

If that is what you're looking for, then you have purchased the wrong book. However, thank you anyway, as I greatly appreciate the royalty payment.

As so much has already been written, why am I adding another book to the large inventory of FBI stories that already exists? Because there is nothing within these previously published works that's very funny. While most law enforcement matters are deadly serious, there's another side to the job that every cop, agent, trooper, investigator, and detective knows is humorous. When we sat around after work in bars and at barbecues, it wasn't the serious work we reminisced about. The conversation always turned to hilarious moments of who did what and to whom. For whatever reason, no one has taken the time to put these lighter moments on paper, or for you millennials, into tiny electrons. Until now.

Here's an example of the kind of story you're in for in the pages ahead:

Another Step Toward Greatness

A student-written, directed, and produced contemporary Greek tragedy was showing at San Diego State University's Don Powell Theatre as part of the Theatre, Television and Film program. One of the lead actors was a large African-American guy. For his commanding performance, he'd dyed his hair blond (think Goldilocks). He was in his early 20s, a hopeful performing arts major at the college. All that stood between him and greatness was the warrant I held in my hands for his arrest.

It seemed my wannabe criminal-actor decided to rob a bank just days before his performance. He had no criminal record and clearly no criminal experience. Note to you readers who are contemplating a life of crime: If you happen to be a 275-pound, dark-skinned African-American male, don't dye your afro bright blond and then walk into a bank with surveillance cameras and witnesses unless you're wearing a disguise. Think hat, mask, anything. However, if you opt to wear a stocking mask, make sure it's not the see-through kind, like another one of my bank robbers wore in a prior case. The sheer nylon—which made his skin appear silky smooth—did nothing to hide his facial features.

Anything that hides your appearance will do. Alas, my bank-robbing thespian hadn't thought ahead, and identifying him was incredibly easy. After all, how many 275-pound Black men with dyed blond hair have you seen in your life? Unless you live in the San Francisco Bay area, these folks tend to not be so common.

INTRODUCTION

So, I tracked my soon-to-be arrestee to the campus theater, where he was performing mid-stage. I made myself comfortable in the audience, as did my FBI partner who had accompanied me on this particular day.

We hadn't been there very long, but I was already bored out of my mind waiting for the dreadful play to end (a "tragedy" in more ways than one). Patron of the arts or not, I couldn't bear it any longer.

I rose from my seat in the middle of the show, and the other agent followed. We politely excused ourselves as we maneuvered around the legs of the seated audience members in our row. Briskly, we worked our way to the back of the theater through the many-mirrored makeup room and around the wings on one side of the stage.

There would be no waiting for a good entrance in this bad play. That much was certain. I walked right onto the stage, confronted the toga-dressed subject and interrupted his soliloquy.

"FBI," I said, identifying myself with the simple letters, then handcuffed him right in the middle of his performance. Without a word of surprise or denial (clearly, he knew why I was there), he oddly said only one thing to me: "Every step I take is another step toward greatness."

As I mentioned, this was supposed to be a Greek tragedy-type play, but my appearance onstage in a requisite FBI Brooks Brothers dark blue suit seemed to have confused the audience. As I exited the stage, with the actor's/subject's hands cuffed behind his back, the audience started to applaud—slowly at first, eventually building to a great ovation. Apparently, most of them believed I was part of the production. On the other hand, maybe they realized I wasn't part of the play, but wanted to thank me for bringing the show to an end.

Once backstage, I was immediately confronted by the student director, who was furious. He claimed I'd ruined his show. I contended, conversely, that having been in the audience myself, the arrest had been the best part of his production yet. The audience obviously concurred.

Filled with pride at my newly discovered and yet-to-be-pursued backup career, I promptly returned to the stage—with prisoner in tow. Before the heavily applauding crowd, I took a brief bow, then exited stage left.

"Every step I take is another step toward greatness," said my subject.

I directed him outside to my Bucar (government speak for "Bureau-issued vehicle"), and my arrestee once again said, "Every step I take is another step toward greatness."

He was such a positive guy, I almost felt bad for arresting him, but police work is not like fishing; there is no catch and release. In the back of my car he would go, then on his way to the federal detention center. My partner got in the driver's seat, and I sat in the backseat behind him with my prisoner beside me on the passenger side.

Even then, the subject was still very positive and upbeat.

As we drove away from the theater, the man with the brilliant golden hair that flowed over his dark skin repeated the words that now live forever in my memory:

"Every step I take is another step toward greatness." And then—as if to confound me more—he added, "This will be good."

As the prospect of going to jail began to sink in, he chose to put a positive spin on his predicament. Large as he was, he said, "I'm going to use my time in prison to get in shape and lose the last fifty pounds."

Not wanting to diminish his positive spirit, I nevertheless interjected to curtail his expectations. "You know, they say the last fifty pounds are always the toughest."

However, sure enough, when his five-year prison stay ended, out he came—in great shape and at least fifty pounds lighter.

After he was released from prison, I don't believe he ever got in trouble again with the law. I think the bank robbery was a whim for him. Something along the lines of, "I need money. Maybe I'll rob a bank." So, he did.

I just happened to be there to co-star in his last theatrical appearance before he took his role to off-off-off-Broadway. On the other hand, it gave him the opportunity to perform for five straight years before an otherwise captive audience. That's a pretty good run for even the best of actors.

Should they have the occasion to meet an FBI agent, most people are in a bit of awe. Television and movies have perpetuated the myth of what it means to be a special agent and the powers of the Bureau. In many cases, this myth is true. Agents are unique people who have the common denominator of being lifetime overachievers, earning good grades in school, being physically fit, and excelling in their work and in other areas of their lives.

But that does not mean they are perfect human beings. As human beings, we all have certain quirks that make us distinctive. Agents, meanwhile, are exposed to a career full of criminals who have their own unusual quirks, personalities, and circumstances to which most people outside law enforcement will never be exposed or get to see. The result of various combinations of elements often creates situations that can be hilarious.

Perhaps intentionally (so as not to disturb the well-established FBI myth), little has been written about this side of the FBI. Trust me, despite what you are about to read, the myth will be just fine. After reading this book, you might even find you like the FBI more.

The work of law enforcement can be gritty—in what you see and with what you come into contact. It's the rare criminal who is properly bathed. A maid has often failed to stop by the home, apparently for years, in advance of a search warrant. In the world of law enforcement, you're exposed to grime in what you see and what you touch. It's the only profession I know where you wash your hands *before* you use the bathroom.

Ask anyone in law enforcement, "What do you like best about your job?" and they won't tell you it was solving crimes, catching criminals, or putting bad guys in jail. They'll tell you it was the people they worked with—which is code for funny stories about what someone did or how they screwed up. Conversely, ask someone in law enforcement, "What didn't you like about your career?" You'll always hear the same answer: "The bureaucracy." As I've said repeatedly since my retirement, "I miss the clowns. I don't miss the circus."

Trust Me

Though some creative license has been taken in how I've decided to share the other stories you're about read, along with a few stories from my police days and my personal life, everything in this book is 100 percent true—to the best of my memory and written records. Nothing has been included from my time practicing law, because honestly, I found no humor in the legal profession. Lawyers rarely smile unless they happen upon a fatal accident.

Also, rest assured that this memoir has been reviewed by the FBI, so there's nothing in here that will compromise national security, though I make no guarantees regarding personal dignity.

Just because nothing in this book is considered *classified* does not mean there are some things that shouldn't be kept private. For example, in certain instances I've changed the names of individuals to protect their identity, or more accurately, their reputation. The last thing I'd ever want to do is reveal someone's true identity— something that might cause them shame and embarrassment. For example, the agent in my book I've named Saul is, in reality, FBI Special Agent Paul Schaff. He might be uncomfortable with some of the things I wrote about him, so for this reason, Paul shall remain anonymous. Forget I even mentioned him.

My goal in writing this book is to educate, inform, and possibly inspire, but most definitely to entertain. Hopefully, those things made it through to the published work you're now reading.

Prior to joining the FBI, I started out as a San Diego police officer. Along the way, I attended law school, then practiced law for a bit before I applied to the Bureau. Because at the time the FBI mostly hired accountants and lawyers, the sole reason I went to law school was to become qualified to apply to the FBI. Nevertheless, changing careers from police officer to lawyer to FBI agent gave me the distinction of having gone from one hated profession to another.

Post-FBI retirement, I'm now a professional speaker and consultant. I still perform work for the FBI occasionally. For a time, they were one of my clients. As soon as I retired, they called and asked me to provide consulting services in some of my areas of expertise on a few special matters. I tried to get out, but they pulled me back in. In this way, trying to leave the FBI is a lot like trying to leave the Mafia. Incidentally, I mean no disrespect to the Mafia.

I began my FBI career in April 1995. After completing the academy's training, I was transferred to my first office, the FBI's Detroit Division. Along with nine other agents, I was assigned to work out of the Flint resident agency (RA), a small satellite office of the Detroit Division about seventy miles north. Some of you may recall the city of Flint from the Michael Moore movie, *Roger and Me*. Let me assure you that Flint was not nearly as glamorous as Hollywood made it out to be.

I was fairly proficient in Spanish, as I'd come to the FBI having worked as a police officer on the streets of San Diego. However, in the wisdom of the federal government, my first assignment as an FBI agent was to be placed as close as possible to the Canadian border.

I spent three years in Flint, although it felt more like twenty-one years—each year there being equivalent to a dog year. Standing on the banks of the Detroit River, Canada was so close I literally could have shot my gun across the river separating our two countries and hit something. Of course, I would have never done such a thing. Likewise, the Canadians were exceptionally nice people who would never consider shooting back. This alone made the Canadians very different from Detroit residents, who used to fire their guns at all times of the day and night for no apparent reason. For a time, Detroiters also had a passion for setting their buildings on fire. I recall one night before Halloween, colloquially referred to as *Devil's Night*, when I was asked to join other agents in standing guard over the federal building to ensure it would still be there in the morning.

While I concerned myself with not being injured (or worse) by the fine citizenry of the greater Detroit metropolis, I also found time for serious work, including the Oklahoma City bombing investigation and a wide variety of other cases, as well as serving on the FBI Detroit SWAT team.

After my transfer from Detroit to the FBI's San Diego Division, I worked violent crimes matters, bank robberies, and kidnappings. I was also among the agents who worked on the September 11 terrorism investigation. Along the way, I must have done a few good things, because the Bureau gave me the FBI Director's Distinguished Service Award for some of my investigative work.

Of course, receiving this award wasn't all because of me; I was fortunate to be assigned good cases and had lots of help from other agents whose work made me look good. Frankly, I was also very lucky to be in the right place at the right time. This availed me the opportunity to work interesting cases and make a string of arrests.

Most agents will transfer to various offices during their careers, and I was no exception. After my tour in San Diego, I was promoted to FBI headquarters in Washington, DC, where I served as the FBI's national spokesperson, addressing the national and international media on all matters that involved the Bureau. This was a demanding albeit relatively thankless job. No matter how hard a law enforcement spokesperson works, it is nearly impossible to get ahead of the media and make your agency look good.

For example, early one morning as I lay in bed asleep, a CNN reporter called my cellphone, waking me up. "This is John," I answered.

"Hey, is it true that Eric Rudolph, the Atlanta Olympic bomber, has been captured?" a woman asked.

"I'm going to be honest," I said. "I'm in bed. You woke me up. Let me look into it and I'll give you a call back." I turned on the TV news and made calls to find out what was going on.

The TV reporter spoke live from her news desk. "I just talked with the spokesperson for the FBI, who reported he was in bed and had not heard anything yet."

I was relieved that I hadn't told her what I was—or rather wasn't—wearing.

Later, I was again promoted. This time it was at FBI headquarters, to the executive staff of the FBI's Cyber Division. When it came to technology, the FBI was entering the twenty-first century kicking and screaming, but it had finally acknowledged that the world was run by computers. The FBI knew it had better develop a way to investigate the cybercrimes that would surely follow.

I was fortunate to have been placed in the Cyber Division at its inception. Sometimes, I worked to help draft laws where none existed. Back then, if you were smart enough to hack into a computer, there were few laws to say you couldn't do such a thing. Nowadays, most kids know enough to hack, but there are a lot of laws that can offer victims at least some protection. Working in the Cyber Division was my first real exposure to the personalities of true cyber geeks, few of whom were actually agents. Many were support employees hired by the FBI because of their skills, none of which apparently included much human interaction. Much like the African Khoisan language, which utilizes clicking sounds for communication as opposed to actual words, I eventually became fluent in interpreting cyber geek grunts, mumblings and lack of direct eye contact to explain complex computer algorithms.

In 2005, I received a promotional transfer to the FBI's Phoenix Division, where I supervised the cyber squad and oversaw all cyber investigations for the state of Arizona. This continued my work with cyber personnel, although they were now typically agents. Most were outgoing, although a few remained social introverts, and now they had guns, which caused me to choose my clicking noises more carefully.

In 2011, I became the assistant special agent in charge of the Phoenix Division, the FBI's No. 2 position for the state of Arizona. In this role, I had accountability for all criminal and cyber investigations, as well as oversight of the FBI's counterintelligence and intel collection programs. During this time, I was awarded an honorary doctorate in computer science from one of Arizona's universities based on some of my contributions to the field of cyber investigations. I didn't let the doctorate go to my head and never insisted that anyone in the office refer to me as doctor, though I did continue to diagnose certain coworkers as crazy.

There was serious work to be done as well. This included working on the Sony computer hack and playing a prominent role in the investigation and aftermath of the shooting of Congresswoman Gabrielle Giffords.

Upon retirement from the FBI I have been pleased to find myself a sought-after speaker. I've enjoyed sharing my unique experiences and intriguing stories, using humor in a way that keeps my audiences informed and entertained. I've presented at hundreds of gatherings and in front of tens of thousands of people, including Fortune 500 companies, domestic and international audiences, the United Nations, etc.; I even presented at the Vatican, where I met with Pope Francis on several occasions.

My meeting with Pope Francis (he is the one on the left).

I handled cyber investigations for many years in the FBI. Whether physical or cyber, security is about protecting you from thieves (bank robbers, forgers, and the like) who want your information or money. Cyber remains a growing trend, and I enjoyed the challenge. How many of you reading this book consider yourself a true cyber geek—meaning you are a technically knowledgeable person? Probably about 1 percent of you.

If you're that kind of person, you're the kind of person I worked with. These were the sort of people who, unlike me, had actually gone to school and earned real doctorates in computer science. Like me, these agents chose to serve their country instead of going out into the private sector to make real money. They were highly skilled and highly technical people.

Even so, some lacked everyday social skills. Some weren't good at small talk. Some were awkward in social situations. Some hadn't kissed a girl. No, that's not true. A few of my agents were lesbians.

They were a great group of people, and besides who am I to judge? I myself have been known to have a few awkward moments now and then—which I'll soon share with you.

The one common denominator in everything I've done in the FBI, as it is with every other special agent, is that it's all about our ability to work with the public. Despite the stoic *X-Files* figures of Mulder and Scully, the FBI agent's job is to talk with people and earn their trust so they'll share what they know. Whether it's helping a victim recall specific details or developing rapport with a subject to gain a confession, the ability to communicate with others and treat them with respect is paramount.

The work, however, is about investigating crimes. It can be a dangerous world. For years, I've sought to convey to my many agents the importance of being friendly while remaining safe with my simple mantra, "Be nice to everyone you meet. But just in case, also have a plan to kill them."

I loved being an FBI agent. It was twenty of the best years of my life.

I joined the Bureau driven by the mission to protect America and its citizens while upholding the Constitution of the United States.

My best memories, however, are of the people I encountered who were interesting and funny, although not everyone intended to be those things.

I wrote this book to share the laughs with you. You now get to read about the moments I experienced during my career. You don't even have to wash your hands before doing so.

Enjoy.

John Iannarelli
FBI Special Agent (Ret.)
1995–2015

The Academy

Every man and woman carrying the badge of a special agent must first have successfully passed through the hallowed halls of the FBI Academy. Located on the grounds of the Marine Corps base in Quantico, Virginia, the academy currently consists of approximately a twenty-week training program where new agent trainees live, eat, and sleep between the classes they attend on the law, countless hours spent on the firing range, and intense physical training (which includes learning hand-to-hand self defense).

Just getting into the FBI Academy is not easy. The Bureau requires applicants to have a four-year degree—most have a master's—and ultimately hires about only one in every 1,000 applicants. To be hired, applicants must be between the ages of twenty-three and thirty-seven; have at least three years' full-time work experience; and be able to pass a written test, an interview, a physical exam, physical fitness test, and polygraph examination. Those with prior criminal histories, even serious motor vehicle violations, need not apply.

Once a new agent trainee arrives at the academy, there is little room for error. Every trainee must pass every test. Written tests require a minimum score of 80 percent. Those who don't score high enough are given a second try, but not scoring 80 percent or above on the second try results in automatic dismissal. Score 80 percent or above on your second try, then not get at least 80 percent on any future test? You're also gone, with no further chances. The same rules apply to grading new agents on the firing range, where they must learn to shoot their Bureau-issued handgun, shotgun, and automatic machine gun. For all practical exercises that score the new agent's ability to subdue uncooperative criminals—supplied by the academy in the form of role players (paid local actors)—applying handcuffs, entering buildings to effect arrests, etc., the same rules apply.

Can A Ticket Be Written Without A License?

A little over twenty-five years ago, I worked as a police officer with the San Diego Police Department prior to reporting for training at the FBI. As there are classes on operating a Bucar during high-speed pursuits and such, all FBI new agent trainees must possess a valid driver's license. Unfortunately, my California driver's license was due to expire when I would later be at the FBI Academy, so I needed to renew my license while I was still in California.

Back then, if you wanted to renew your California license prior to its expiration, you couldn't just expect to have a new license issued upon request. No, because it is the government at work (and not just any government, but the California government), the powers that be sought to complicate the process as much as humanly possible. Hence, California required that you take the written test again, even though you held a currently valid driver's license.

Just so we are absolutely clear: If your license is due to expire and you do nothing, it will automatically renew without any sort of test, whether you know the rules of the road or not. However, if you wish to renew your license early (for example, you'll be out of state during the time it's set to expire), it is necessary to showcase a license holder's written test-taking skills. It makes no sense to me, but show me something in California that does.

After I explained my predicament to my San Diego P.D. sergeant, he kindly told me to take a break while I was on duty, drive a couple of miles away to the closest Department of Motor Vehicles office, and get myself a new license. So, I answered a few radio calls, and when things appeared to be quiet, I drove to the DMV—in full police uniform and in a marked police vehicle. Enjoying the parking privileges of being a cop while I still could (which necessitates keeping your car close by should there be a need to depart quickly in an emergency), I parked in front of the DMV in the red *No Parking* area, walked right into the DMV, strode confidently up to the counter, and spoke with the first available able-bodied government representative.

I explained my situation to the worker. She confirmed I must retake the written test.

No problem, I thought. *I am ready and prepared.*

For the past few years, I'd passed out tickets to drivers who clearly did not know the rules of the road. I took the paper test and pencil from her with no concerns and found myself a seat at a nearby table. Yes, I was a bit cocky, but I had good reason to be. Not only was I charged to enforce the rules of the road, I was now en route to the highest of all law enforcement academies: the FBI.

I raced through the test in a minute or two, finishing well within the allotted time, then returned to the counter, whereupon the government minion graded my test. I failed.

In my rush to complete the test, I apparently didn't read the questions closely enough and made stupid mistakes. Be that as it may, in a display of power that was probably the only reason she liked her job, the representative proceeded to cut my license in half, right in front of me.

There I was, a sworn police officer who wrote tickets for a living, standing in uniform at the DMV with his marked police car parked out front, and suddenly I had no license. As if this wasn't bad enough, she then informed me there was a mandatory waiting period before I could retake the test. I should return in two weeks!

I can't go to the FBI Academy without a driver's license.

I can't even go back to work as a police officer without a driver's license.

I can't go back to the police station without driving my police car!

I pleaded to speak with her supervisor, and once appeased, I explained the situation. This appeared to have little effect.

Without missing a beat, I switched from logic to begging. The supervisor finally relented. I would be allowed to retake a redacted test.

"Look," she said. "I'm gonna ask you one question. If you answer this question correctly, I'll grant you your driver's license."

Everything was now on the line. I didn't want to be the first FBI agent in history to report to the academy for training after having my police car towed away for both illegal parking and operating a vehicle without a license.

Lay it on me! I thought.

"What is the minimum blood alcohol content you can have as an eighteen-year-old and still operate a vehicle?" she asked.

Aha! It's a trick question! Thank you, God!

"You can't have alcohol in your system," I said, "because you're only eighteen and the legal drinking age is twenty-one."

"Correct," she replied. "You pass."

I got my new driver's license, departed faster than I had arrived, and drove directly back to the police station. Two weeks later, I was at the FBI Academy.

I've never shared this story with anyone. Until now.

My days as a police officer with a valid driver license.

A Pretty Ugly Ticket

As I mentioned previously, I wrote my fair share of tickets while I was a police officer. I've heard most of the excuses people have tried to avoid receiving one. Some of the approaches drivers used were not very subtle. As you can imagine, they received an equally unsubtle response from me.

One time, I pulled over a driver for speeding who turned out to be an attractive young woman. In her attempt to flirt her way out of a ticket, she said: "I thought the police didn't give tickets to pretty girls."

"We don't," I said. "Sign here."

Trigger-Pull Test

One of the first things you have to do before arriving at the academy is prove you can pull the trigger on a gun. This may sound fairly easy to most people, but for some it can be difficult. A trigger has a certain amount of pull, measured in poundage, as in a five-pound trigger pull is akin to lifting five pounds—with just your index finger. It may be easy once or twice, but can you keep pulling the trigger, over and over again if necessary, until you've stopped someone who's trying to harm you or someone else?

As a police officer, carrying a gun was part of my job. I'd walk around with one on my hip all day, not to mention having to regularly qualify to carry my weapon. I practiced often to stay proficient. Like the driver's license renewal, I expected the trigger-pull test to present me with no difficulty. It's another step in the government's one-size-fits-all vetting process, but I was well-prepared.

My kindly sergeant once again allowed me to take time off during work to drive my marked patrol car to the FBI office, in uniform, to prove I could pull the trigger of a gun.

Once there, I met with the office firearms instructor. He showed me that the weapon was unloaded and safe and then handed me the gun. I pointed my arm out straight with the empty weapon facing a target on the wall.

I then pulled the trigger as many times as I could until I was told to stop. I probably pulled the trigger fifty times in less than a minute. Clearly, I passed the test.

At the academy, you have to be able to shoot with either hand. After all, if you injure your shooting hand during a gunfight, you still need to be able to defend yourself shooting with your non-gun hand (otherwise known as your weak hand). Not too long ago, a trainee showed up at the FBI Academy for training who couldn't shoot with both hands. Not because he wasn't strong enough. He was former military special forces and had exactly the characteristics you'd expect to find in an excellent FBI agent. Unfortunately, this new agent trainee had been injured prior to arriving at the academy and had lost one of his hands. He now relied on the use of a prosthetic.

Most agents who met this trainee agreed they would rather have him at their side than some agents with regular hands who couldn't perform nearly as well. Nevertheless, despite his strong suitability, he had 50 percent fewer hands than required by the academy and some government employee in a position of authority thought this recruit should not be permitted to become an agent. This eventually resulted in a civil suit, which raised protection concerns from the Americans with Disabilities Act. This new agent trainee would eventually win his battle with the government. Once he was allowed to complete new agent training, he successfully served the Bureau.

For a while, the Americans with Disabilities Act opened up opportunities to others who wanted to be FBI agents, but weren't nearly as suitable for the job. People started showing up at the FBI Academy who weren't in good enough shape to complete many of the physical requirements.

One candidate couldn't even complete the required two-mile run, let alone do it in the required time. Completing the two-mile run is considered the bare minimum acceptable for the FBI physical fitness test. I totally understand and agree with the importance of making reasonable accommodations for people whenever possible, but you have to draw the line somewhere. I might have wanted to play in the NBA, but they wouldn't let me use a step ladder. Eventually, things settled back to normal, and worthy exceptions to the standardized rules were made on a case-by-case basis.

Speaking of shooting, one of our academy classmates appeared to be a very suitable candidate, but for some reason or another had difficulty hitting the target in firearms training. She did fine when we practiced, but as soon as the instructors announced we'd be graded on our shooting, she become so stressed her performance level dropped. She worked for the post office before joining the FBI. In light of all the post office employees going *postal at the time*, most of us thought everyone who worked at the post office could shoot. She might have been the lone exception.

Given enough practice, shooting is a skill that can be developed and improved. Unfortunately, a new agent trainee is only afforded so much time and practice, and it didn't appear she would make it. That is until...

Another classmate and I stood on either side of her at the firing range facing our targets and conspired to help her pass. It was our final shooting qualification, and we agreed each of us would sacrifice a few rounds by purposely aiming to put our bullets through her target. The other agent and I were good shooters, so rather than earning a perfect score of 100 (two points for each of the fifty rounds put through the target), we'd settle with a satisfactory but passing score so our classmate would be able to graduate. It was the perfect plan, until the instructors scored the heretofore less-than-adequate former postal employee a 116! While the other agent and I put four rounds each through the center of her target, she had pulled herself together enough to earn a perfect score on her own.

The other agent and I were advised we needed more practice as we had both missed our targets entirely with several rounds each, and even inadvertently struck another agent's target. No good deed ever goes unpunished, so our altruistic plan earned both of us a few more hours on the range after the rest of the class was dismissed for the day—including the agent we tried to help.

You Missed A Spot

There are myriad tasks in which the academy seeks to make new agent trainees proficient. Surely, the FBI spares no expense when it comes to providing high-quality training for those who would be called a special agent. Or perhaps the government is just cutting costs elsewhere? The government is very good about hiring people with disabilities whenever it can. As part of the federal government, the FBI takes providing an equal opportunity for employment seriously when it hires individuals with physical challenges. Much like the rest of the government, while the heart may be in the right place, the head is often anatomically elsewhere. More on this in a moment.

There is no more frequented facility at the FBI Academy than the gym. It comprises large cardio rooms, weight rooms, floor areas, and the locker rooms, which have showers and restrooms. Physical training is not only required and tested at the academy, it's also part of the FBI culture.

FBI agents are expected to remain in good physical shape throughout their careers. They're even afforded one hour while on duty, three days a week, to work out. This is all done to maintain peak physical conditioning. Agents are tested twice a year on their physical fitness. This includes pushups, sit-ups, running, etc., so working out regularly is essential. Agents who can't pass the physical fitness test risk losing part of their income, and quite possibly, their job. The importance of exercising regularly is instilled throughout new agent training.

During my time in the academy, one of the physical training tests we had to complete was the shuttle run. This test consisted of lying on our backs on the gymnasium floor. Upon hearing the instructor blow the whistle, trainees roll onto their stomachs, launch themselves forward and onto their feet, then race across the gym floor between a series of cones. After reaching one end of the gym, they turn around, race all the way back, then turn around again and complete the full distance run one more time. The entire distance was only 120 yards, but starting from a position on the floor and lying on your back while having to change directions multiple times, which invariably slowed the runner down, made this a very competitive event to complete in the allotted time of a maximum of twenty-five seconds.

When my turn came, I eagerly dropped to the ground. While doing so, I struck the back of my head hard against the gym floor. It was one of those hard smacks where, if I'd been in the NFL, they'd have taken me out of the game. Through the headache haze and dizziness, I heard from somewhere what sounded like a whistle signaling my start of the graded fit test.

Somehow, I forced myself off the floor and took off running. Like a drunk person, I made much wider turns around the cones than necessary. I'd apparently struck my head so hard that I had trouble running. Judging distances was out of the question. I finished, though, and did it in 24.9 seconds. Only one-tenth of a second stood between finishing the shuttle run successfully and graduating from the FBI Academy. Another tenth of a second and you would not be reading this book.

For those who are already agents, such as the administration and instructors at the academy, physical exercise is even more prevalent than in the field. Barring some sort of injury, anyone assigned to work at the academy will find themselves in the gym for some part of the day. It's how agents at the academy are wired. In their mentality, it's no different from taking time every day to eat lunch.

With so many people passing through a communal gymnasium each day, using the restrooms and shower facilities, you can understand why maintaining the building's physical cleanliness is essential. The last thing the FBI wants is to spread germs and make anyone sick. One would think this would be obvious to everyone and require some, albeit minimal, consideration.

That's what I thought, too, until one day when I was in the men's locker room, when entered a government cost-cutting measure. Minding my own business, I was struck unexpectedly from behind on the back of my legs with what I assumed was a stick. When I half-turned, I saw a blind man with dark glasses and a cane, the instrument that had struck me. In his other hand, he held a mop. This blind man was the men's locker room janitor. He was blind, so I guess he could have been assigned to the women's locker room as well, but that's not the point.

The blind man apologized and stated he had not known anyone was present as he was "feeling" his way through his cleaning chores.

Yes, you read that correctly: feeling his way through his locker room-cleaning chores.

No offense to anyone sight-impaired, but really, how much thought went into the logic behind this person's work assignment? If I were to tell him he missed a spot, what could he do about it? In the world of the government, this made perfect sense. The blind janitor would keep his job at the academy.

Incidentally, not long afterward, the academy gym locker rooms were declared to be contaminated with the MRSA virus and had to be closed for approximately eighteen months while the government contracted out cleaning and repairs. To date, I'm not sure anyone's been able to determine how the contamination could have possibly occurred.

And, while the academy was determined to save pennies on the cleaning crew, they were finding new ways to lose millions of dollars.

One agent assigned to the academy wanted to truly impress his co-worker girlfriend with a special marriage proposal. He persuaded one of the Bureau's helicopter pilots to swoop down low and hover close by just feet off the ground as the couple were out for a walk and he knelt to propose. Unfortunately, the helicopter pilot scraped the tail rotor on the ground, causing the helicopter to crash. Fortunately, everyone escaped serious injury, although the multi-million dollar helicopter was totaled. Still, it turned out to be a memorable marriage proposal.

Even after graduating from the FBI Academy, agents continued to enhance their educational training through what the Bureau refers to as *in-services*. This is when agents report back to the academy and spend a week or so receiving advanced training on whatever topic is deemed appropriate for their careers. If you're selected for the SWAT team, you're sent to the academy for SWAT training.

SWAT teams are made up of individuals who are tough in both strength and personality. A sign of weakness is frowned upon, and anything seen as less than cool and self-confident is dealt with immediately by what is euphemistically referred to as the Kangaroo

Court, where senior SWAT team members assemble and decide on an appropriate punishment for perceived violations. Violations of lessor offenses, but equally punishable, might typically include wearing a hat that offended the sensibilities of the SWAT team leader (hint: it is important to know college rivalries and where your team leader went to school). Punishment for a lesser offense could range from the guilty party having to purchase drinks for everyone during the next social outing to physical punishment like pushups. One evening after a day of training, the SWAT team gathered at a steakhouse for dinner. Drinks were ordered all around. Perhaps the drink one agent ordered had a more generic name at his local tavern, but when the waitress arrived with a tray full of beverages and asked, "Who gets the Sassy Cowgirl?" the Kangaroo Court was immediately called to order.

Lawyers will spend a couple of weeks attending in-service training being taught the art of looking after the FBI's legal interests. The same thing goes for accountants and everyone else. About once a year, on average, an agent can expect to return to Quantico for a period of in-service learning. As I approached retirement, I began to add up the weeks of training I'd attended at the FBI Academy. It turned out I'd spent more than a year of my life living in the FBI's dormitory.

Not all in-service training is conducted at the academy. Often, agents will travel to a city where a hotel and conference room are leased out for the training. This is usually done when the academy is full of those undergoing new agent training, or when the allure of the academy was not enough to convince more senior agents to return.

For one such training class, I found myself in Lansing, Michigan, staying at the Amway Hotel, a lavish hotel in a lavish location that had clearly been financed through the sale of door-to-door products. The training itself would turn out to be nothing particularly significant, but even so, we'd been cautioned not to identify ourselves as FBI agents upon arrival. Even the signs leading to the hotel training room were somewhat inconspicuous, not remotely indicating that the FBI was present. As it turned out, MUFON (Michigan UFO Network) was holding its annual conference at the same hotel, and government officials were concerned the coincidence of the FBI being present at the same time would be viewed by some as a conspiracy.

On the last night of the conference, feeling somewhat lonesome for home, I decided to wander to the hotel bar and sit by myself at a table. I watched a game on TV and slowly nursed a drink. I didn't see anyone else I knew who had attended the training class, but noted a number of UFO society members whom I'd observed during the week chatting nearby. One person in particular caught my attention. He explained to his fellow society members that he was not a conspiracy theorist, but simply didn't believe the US government was sharing everything it knew with its citizens.

As I listened to this man, I couldn't help but become empathetic to what he was saying. I, too, was a concerned citizen who wanted my government to be forthright and open. While not a UFO enthusiast myself, I suspected that, on other matters, there might be those in power who don't share certain information because it was assumed the American people could not handle the truth. With thoughts like these in common, I wondered if I should consider the whole UFO thing more deliberately. After all, as Scully and Mulder say, "The truth is out there."

Just as I was about to become a believer, the man I'd overheard turned to one of the other people at his table and said, "So, Bob. Tell us about your abduction."

They'd been so close to recruiting a new believer, but with that, I snapped back to reality, finished my drink, and called it a night.

Something Is Bugging The Assistant Director

The FBI Academy is overseen by an assistant director who has authority over all aspects of FBI training and functions to be carried out. The FBI Academy is considered to be the bastion of knowledge, heralded throughout law enforcement as being no finer a place on planet Earth from which law enforcement personnel emerge.

Many roles are served at the academy, the most obvious of which is the training of new FBI special agents, more commonly known as new agent trainees, and even more commonly known as NATs, once again embracing the government's love of acronyms.

The assistant director believed it was important to demonstrate his level of intellect while also proving to everyone that they were there to support the interests of those of us on the lowest of levels. This particular assistant director took great offense to the acronym NATs, believing it trivialized the importance of these young trainees. In a selfless act of both independence and bravery, the assistant director decided to take a stand. He crafted an email to personally send to all people who attended, were assigned to, or in any way did business with the FBI Academy.

To hold himself even further accountable to the mission of showing respect to all, the assistant director copied his email to the FBI director and others within the upper echelon of the Bureau, letting them know he had taken this stand:

Commencing immediately, from this point forward,
new agent trainees will no longer be described as such

in writing using the abbreviation NATs. These are some of the brightest and most self-sacrificing people who exist. These individuals who have decided to dedicate their professional lives in the service of the FBI must and will be treated with respect at all times, on all levels by all persons. They will no longer be referred to as NATs, needlessly equating them with a tiny bug.

A brave agent hit the reply all button and responded with the simple message: "Gnat is spelled with a 'G.'"

Accidental Awkwardness

The FBI's National Academy is a training program offered to high-ranking police officers from all over the world. Later during my career, I returned to the academy and for ten weeks I lived with more than 250 of these officers as one of their FBI agent counselors. My job was to assist with the training program to ensure their success. I had officers from big cities, small towns, and abroad, where English was not their native language. One Southern good ol' boy was the nicest person you'd ever want to meet. He wouldn't call me *Agent* or *John*, but just like on the old *Waltons* television series, he'd call me *John Boy*. As a matter of fact, he'd add *Boy* to just about everyone's name. I'd often hear *John Boy* or *Mark Boy* or *Joe Boy*, etc. This added a sort of pleasant familiarity to our encounters.

All was fine until one day during lunch in the FBI Academy cafeteria. Hundreds of police officers, new agents in training, and even a small delegation of law enforcement visiting from Israel were in attendance. That's when my Southern officer called out across the cafeteria to his Korean classmate Mr. Joo (pronounced Jew), *Hey, Joo Boy! Come over here!*

I thought my time at the academy couldn't end soon enough.

Hell Week

At the halfway point during academy training, the class of new agent trainees passed through Hell Week, a five-day period when the class would be subjected to a series of tests—written, on the gun range, physical fitness, and defensive tactic skills. Successful completion of this week generally guaranteed one would make it through to graduation, and on the last day of Hell Week agents were rewarded by receiving their future office assignments.

During this FBI rite of passage, the new agent trainees gathered in their main classroom with their instructors seated in the back of the room. On a desk in the front of the room lay a pile of white envelopes, one envelope for each new agent trainee. Each agent's name was typed on the front, and the agent's orders to where they would report after graduation were sealed inside.

In this tradition, one new agent trainee would be selected at random and given his or her envelope. The trainee would stand before the class, announce where they're from, where they wanted to go, and where they thought the Bureau would be sending them. The trainee would then open the envelope and read where they were being sent. Upon hearing the good news, the class would break into applause and congratulate their fellow classmate. Meanwhile, an instructor would hand the trainee a Bureau photo of the new agent, which the agent would then pin on a wall map of the country indicating the city where they'd been assigned. To complete the cycle, the agent would then pick a random envelope from the pile and call out the trainee's name appearing on the envelope. This process was repeated until everyone had their assignment.

About two-thirds of the way through the envelope pile, my name was called. I anxiously made my way to the front of the classroom. Gripping my envelope, I proudly announced I had processed into the FBI from San Diego, but I wanted to try something new by going to the East Coast. I hoped for the Richmond Division, but assumed that, because of my police work in San Diego and my skills in speaking street Spanish, the Bureau would return me to San Diego. I opened my envelope and—for what seemed like an eternity—stared at my orders. One of my classmates snapped a photo for posterity. Years later, the photo still reveals that all color had drained from my face.

Finally, I read my assignment out loud. I was being sent to the Flint RA, out of the FBI's Detroit Division. I had no idea where this was and needed help finding the proper place to pin my photo to the map.

There would be no East Coast or Southern charm. No returning to the warmth of San Diego. I, a newly graduated FBI agent, would soon be reporting to Flint, Michigan—one of the most violent cities in America, with temperatures that dropped to as low as forty below zero with the wind chill factor. I soon realized this would be a far more challenging and demanding assignment than I had anticipated. Nonetheless, I figured a bad day in the field would be better than a good day in the academy. I could not wait.

Signs posted just outside of the Academy gym warning those who enter what to expect.

The Agents

FBI agents are the backbone of the Bureau. Of the 35,000 FBI employees, there are approximately 12,000 highly educated, extensively trained, and hard-working special agents. They regularly make sacrifices and often risk their lives to protect others. Each person is a fascinating individual, and each comes from varied experiences and walks of life.

And yet, there is always that one agent who makes you shake your head and say, *How in the world did* that person *get hired?*

Gym Application

Like most FBI offices, I discovered the Detroit Division had its own gym, where agents could work out during the day. The Flint RA office was small and had no room for a gym, so I had to purchase my own membership at a local health club. In the end, it probably worked out in my favor, as having my own membership prevented me from exposing myself to an embarrassing setup.

One ingenious Detroit Division agent decided to make up a fake gym membership application for the new agents reporting in to the office for their first assignment. This application had all the basic questions—name, address, and the requisite fine print no one ever reads when joining a gym, like *I promise to replace all weights and other equipment after use*, or *I promise to limit the use of cardio machines to only thirty minutes during peak hours when other persons are waiting.* The Detroit prankster, however, added a few extra lines you won't find on your average gym application: *I promise not to stare too long at any one particular person while they are in the shower or otherwise in a state of undress.*

Of course, new agents do as they're told, and they readily affixed their photographs as required and signed these fake gym membership applications. The questionable sections of these applications were later highlighted, and copies were hung on various office bulletin boards.

After seeing a few of these, I immediately went home and checked the fine print on my health club membership.

Bunny Boiler

I planned to attend a black-tie event that would be put on by the alumni of my law school. Despite having requested the day off from work, I was called in by my squad supervisor to assist with the impending arrest of a serial bank robber.

The case agent handling the bank robbery investigation was a female squad member who was known to be, shall we say, high-strung. It was her case, but a matter like this required the assistance of everyone on the squad, so without hesitation and despite having prior plans, I headed into the office. First, however, I put my tux in the back of my Bucar. If the day lasted too long, something I couldn't predict, I planned for a worst-case scenario where I could change at work and drive directly to the event.

As the day wore on, the serial bank robber was eventually arrested. This led to all the necessities of properly interviewing him, processing him into the system, and taking him to the federal jail. It so happened that the female case agent also had big plans for the evening, which apparently involved a first date with some new guy. Aside from a being assigned to a serial bank robbery, she also was a serial dater, never holding on to one relationship before the man of the hour, day, or week wisely decided to move on.

The arrest was her case, but she disappeared, leaving myself and another agent to handle all the post-arrest work. I ended up missing my black-tie event, along with losing the money I had paid to attend. I was annoyed but decided to let it go. Who am I to stand in the way of someone trying to find their soulmate? After all, based on her dating volume, she must have been getting close to running out of unused souls.

As I sat in the squad area a few days later, this same agent (who, despite my having done her a huge favor handling the processing of her arrestee, had never thanked me), leaned across the cubical separating us and started yelling at me. She was angry because she felt I didn't do a proper and thorough post-arrest interview of her subject.

Did I understand her properly? She was angry because she didn't believe I'd done a good enough job doing work—her work—that she skipped out on?

Bunny Boiler was screaming at me. That's what she was referred to in the office, as an homage to Glenn Close's character in the 1987 thriller movie *Fatal Attraction*. This should give you a mild indication of who I had to deal with.

As she continued screaming in my squad-area cubical, I discreetly lifted the receiver off my desk telephone and pressed number 4. This put the phone into speaker mode and simultaneously activated the office's overhead paging system. Now everyone in the office, on every single floor, in every nook and cranny of the building, could hear what was going on.

I just sat there stone-faced. The longer I sat there, the further immersed she became in her semipsychotic state, saying all sorts of terrible things as she vented her unwarranted but very real anger. To her audience, she sounded a bit ridiculous as she complained that *her* work had not been performed by me to her satisfaction.

After she'd apparently expended all of her available energy (and, for the moment, had exorcised all her personal demons), I just sat there. I didn't yell back.

I took a moment of pause, perhaps intentionally, to build the anticipation for my listening audience. Finally, I replied: "Every time you yell at me like that, when you criticize me, when you are unappreciative of me...I become so aroused."

After Bunny Boiler was shocked into silence for a moment, she screamed and stormed out of the office. She later made a formal complaint that I had caused her professional embarrassment, which fell on deaf ears (unlike her overheard office tirade). Ultimately, she resigned from the Bureau. I'm not sure what she's doing now, but I'm guessing she doesn't work as a life coach.

Fat, Smart, And Happy

Since the inception of the FBI, the Bureau has relentlessly insisted agents maintain their state of peak physical fitness, pass their annual medical exam, and successfully complete the twice-a-year fitness test. The failure of any of these can lead to a reduction of salary by as much as 25 percent, and quite possibly, the loss of an agent's job.

Despite these consequences, there are some who struggle with the battle of the bulge.

A story known throughout the Bureau occurred during the Hoover years. An agent had gotten terribly out of shape, to the point he was considered obese. Word was out that the Bureau was cracking down on those *unfit* for duty. If this agent could not pass his next physical examination (with height and weight in proper proportion), he'd be terminated.

The agent knew he could never lose enough weight before his scheduled medical exam, but he wasn't really interested in getting into shape, anyway. He was eligible to retire in less than six months, so what he really needed to do was figure out a way to hang on to his job just a little while longer.

As the story goes, the agent went to a men's clothing store, where he purchased a suit and shirt many sizes too large, then made an appointment to meet personally with the director of the FBI.

Wearing his extra-large suit, he arrived at his appointment and told the director he'd become so motivated by the Bureau's new edict that agents must pass their physicals that he'd fully applied himself to the mission of getting into shape. The agent went on to explain that, as a result, he'd already lost a tremendous amount of weight and was continuing to do so, which is why his clothes were so baggy now. The agent explained his doctor had advised him that, for the safety of his health, he needed to slow down on the weight loss. The agent explained he expected to be at his ideal weight in a little more than six months.

Director Hoover, duly impressed by the success of this agent's apparent weight loss, gave the agent a six-month extension before he had to take his next physical. Just enough time for the agent to then promptly retire, fat and happy.

Fascinating And Quirky

When I was in the FBI, I worked with a rocket scientist who'd been employed by NASA, a colleague who had been a doctor, numerous former lawyers, and many who were former successful businessmen and businesswomen. The FBI continues to attract some of the greatest minds. That does not necessarily eliminate the quirky ones. Among all FBI agents, some can be, shall we say, excessively frugal.

You may prefer to call them *cheap*. Most agents are proud of this attribute. No one will become rich working for the government, so you have to be resourceful with what little money you earn. Being frugal is one thing, but while some agents wear their stinginess like a badge of honor, some have achieved new heights in their low income.

A group of agents were plucked from the San Diego Division to work a surveillance assignment. They faced a two-hour drive to the destination and were provided a per diem by the FBI for travel expenses. This was a dollar amount the government had determined an agent would require to purchase meals and sleep in an acceptable hotel. The food and hotel money could be spent as we'd like, and if any money was left over, agents could keep the difference. Over time, this could add up. But as this would only be a weeklong assignment, no one planned to get rich. Except, perhaps, for one agent.

Upon arrival, while the rest checked into a modest hotel and took their meals at a local restaurant, this particular agent procured much cheaper accommodations—the backseat of his Bucar. In lieu of spending his per diem on a hotel, he thought it would be more profitable to sleep in his government car and shower at a nearby military facility (to which he'd been permitted access). Thank goodness for that, because I'm sure he'd otherwise have just gone without bathing.

This agent's financial ingenuity did not stop there. While the rest of the agents were wasting their government-issued money on unnecessary luxuries like cooked food, this agent had bought himself a jar of peanut butter and a box of crackers, which he'd determined would be his daily rations for the duration of the stay. Clearly, this was someone who knew how to stretch a dollar.

Shortly after the surveillance assignment ended I had been transferred out of the San Diego Division, and was at FBI headquarters in Washington, DC. I hadn't seen or thought about this agent for years. But as I walked the FBI headquarters hallways, I was passed by the agent—who was riding a Razor scooter inside the building. Most agents don't get a Bucar while at headquarters, so I had the feeling that, rather than spend money to purchase a car, this was his economical and primary mode of transportation. The Razor scooter-riding agent was not the only frugal one I encountered in the FBI.

When a large contingent of agents was summoned to Long Island, New York, to assist in collecting parts from an airliner crash, one industrious agent decided to capitalize on the per diem, which was several hundred dollars a day for a hotel and food. The agents would be there for at least a couple of months. A modest hotel in the New York area at the time would be at least $200 a night, but instead of checking into such a hotel, this particular agent found himself a nearby campground where he could pitch a tent for a dollar per evening. By the end of the assignment, I think he came back home with a little more than $10,000 profit.

Agents could get very creative with their finances when it came to using the government credit card. For example, upon leaving the academy, each new FBI agent is issued a government Mastercard—to be used only for work-related travel expenses, food, and accommodations. The agent could use it to pay for dinner at a restaurant, a hotel, or in the aforementioned cases, to spend the evening at a campsite. Otherwise, the use of government credit is off limits. At the end of travel, the agent would submit an invoice with receipts and be reimbursed, and was expected to immediately pay their government credit card bill in full.

A select few agents short on cash, have been known to use the government credit card, thinking they'll pay the bill when it arrives. Who would ever know?

The government, that's who.

The government employs civil service accounting drones who receive copies of the agents' credit card bills and review those bills in search of violations of the terms of use. When a violation occurs, it's reported to the agent's supervisor, who is then tasked to determine the reason for the violation. There is generally no problem if it was an honest mistake and the agent accidentally used the wrong card. If the agent knowingly used the government credit card, there may be an issue. The greater the violation, the greater the issue.

One such violation that came my way involved an agent who used his government credit card to pay for an ocean cruise. I assumed this would fall into the *I mistakenly used the wrong credit card category*, so I called the agent into my office and asked what happened. To my surprise, the agent told me paying for the cruise with the card had not been an error.

Was it some sort of undercover operation with which I was not familiar? No. The agent explained he'd had plenty of money to cover the travel expense, and when the bill arrived, he would pay it in full, but he couldn't use his personal credit card. I asked him why not.

The agent explained he and his girlfriend would be taking the cruise, but the personal credit card statements would be reviewed by his wife and he didn't want her to know. He was in violation of the rules of FBI conduct, but at least he had a plan.

Have You Seen My Dye Pack?

I'd been in the FBI for a few years, stationed in San Diego. I was enjoying the kind of excitement one expects to find in a career as a special agent. I responded to bank robberies and on the way would always keep an eye out for the robbers who'd just fled the scene of the crime. This was just the sort of excitement I'd signed up for. However, sometimes the excitement had nothing to do with an actual crime.

I'd just arrived at the scene of a bank robbery. Bank employees were there, as were a few customers who'd witnessed the crime and some other agents who were investigating.

Apparently, the victim in question was a bank teller who'd handed the bank robber a stack of money with a concealed dye pack designed to explode about thirty seconds after the robber exits the bank. It's triggered when an electronic signal is tripped by the dye pack passing through the bank doors. When a dye pack bursts, it releases a red dye chemical that stains the money, the robber, and anything else in the immediate vicinity. The red dye chemical also contains a type of tear gas, which further incapacitates the robber. However, for some reason, this dye pack didn't detonate.

While agents were investigating, one of the squad agents walked inside the bank and said, "Hey, look what I found." He had a wad of cash. "I found this in the parking lot."

BOOM!

Money swirled around the agent like his own little tornado. He was covered in red dye and succumbing to the side effects of the tear gas—burning and watery eyes, breathing problems, excessive saliva, and skin irritation—as were most of the rest of us inside the bank, including the bank employees and customer witnesses. Apparently, when the robber left the bank, he ditched the money in the parking lot when he discovered what he'd been handed. The lucky agent, on the other hand, who didn't know about the dye pack in the money, confirmed what no one had ever wondered: dye packs can be triggered when entering a bank, as well as when exiting one.

During a different robbery, a dye pack given to a bank robber by the bank teller exploded in the robber's possession. Although he'd successfully made it out of the bank, the resulting dye and tear gas made him ill, and he'd vomited in the bank's parking lot.

I will never forget the immortal words of my squad supervisor: "Get a vomit sample in case we can pull any DNA out of it, and while you're at it, clean the rest of this up."

So that's what I did. In my nice suit with rubber gloves, I picked up vomit-ridden money. It should be duly noted that none of this was in any of the FBI recruiting brochures when I applied to become a special agent.

Benefit Of The Doubt

Every FBI office utilizes duty agents, a revolving roster of agents whose job for the day is to remain at the office and be available for any citizen who calls or walks into the FBI office to make a complaint. Most agents dread their duty agent days because it takes time away from their assigned cases. Plus, since I served as the duty agent on many occasions, I can personally attest that many of those impulsive complaint people are just crazy.

Think about it. If you have an important matter worthy of FBI attention, do you just grab some boxes filled with papers you believe to be evidence and show up unannounced, or do you call first and set up an appointment?

One of my walk-in complainers wanted the FBI's help because the US military had purportedly stolen his idea for a submarine, the diagrams for which he had hand-drawn and brought in to show me. His diagrams were immaculate. They displayed the skill of a professional mechanical engineer and depicted detailed designs. What made his submarine unique, however, was that it had wheels. He explained it was to be a land-based vehicle.

I was never able to comprehend why this walk-in didn't realize his design was actually known as a bus, or why he believed the military had stolen his idea. Regardless, whenever he saw any sort of bus pass him by, he was convinced the military had robbed him of his invention and the accompanying design profits. I told him I'd be on the lookout for any submarines on the freeway and would contact him once we got to the bottom of the matter.

For the duty agent, phone calls could be far crazier than walk-ins. Many people rambled their anger at the government, their neighbors, or anything else that came into their minds. As an FBI duty agent, you couldn't just hang up, even if you knew the person on the other end of the phone to be questionably sane. Crazy or not, they might also be a taxpayer, and we at the FBI were here to serve the public.

I had to endure many of these time-wasting calls, even when there wasn't a specific complaint or anything of value that needed to be addressed. After a while, I employed a new tactic. After the caller had droned on for about ten minutes, I cut them off to interrupt. "Excuse me," I'd say. "I hate to interrupt, but you think you have problems? Listen to this!"

I would then begin to regale the caller with everything going on in my life—the demands of working for the FBI, raising a family, living paycheck to paycheck, the unusually dark-colored growth of a mole on some obscure part of my body that I really needed have looked at by a doctor, etc. More times than not, the caller would become bored and hang up on me. Problem solved.

It's worth noting that these calls could also have serious consequences as well. One time, when I was a supervisor, one of my agents called in sick, and it happened to be her turn as the duty agent. How convenient.

Anyway, being the nice supervisor that I was, and for old times' sake, I figured, *What the heck. I'm sitting here working at my desk anyway. I'll answer the duty agent phone calls.*

However, after a couple of time-wasting calls, I'd had enough for the day. Like any good supervisor, I delegated the remainder of the duty agent responsibility to one of my other agents. As much fun as I'd had speaking with loopy callers, I was really too busy to allow myself to continue. With the fit test looming just over the horizon, I really needed to get my workout in. And, of course, there was lunch.

The delegated agent was a stellar example of what you look for in an FBI agent. He took his work seriously. Sure enough, shortly after I passed the duty agent torch to him, a crazy call came in. What did my agent do? He took the radical approach of listening to the caller for thirty minutes, and then the call ended—most likely because the caller had grown hoarse from talking so much.

My agent, however, went on to display a level of thoroughness that bordered on OCD—in a good way. The agent ran a computer check on the caller, which included pulling up the caller's photograph from driver's license records. The agent then contacted the police in the caller's hometown and let them know there was a disturbed individual who lived in their jurisdiction whom they might come across at some point in the future.

Two days later, the same caller barricaded himself inside his house and fired a gun randomly at a passersby. Thanks in part to my agent's competence and concern, the police knew exactly who the shooter was and were able to resolve the situation without anyone getting hurt. All in all, I still think my problems were worse at the time. At least I got my workout in.

For Sale

When I worked in the Flint RA, agents didn't have an individual desk phone number. Rather, there was just one main number for the small office of agents.

One agent assigned to Flint always seemed to be clearing out his garage and selling something: his lawn mower, a stereo, old golf clubs—all sorts of things. He didn't own an answering machine (this was before voicemail on home phones was a standard feature). Rather than use his home phone number in the local newspaper want ads, concerned he'd miss a call from a potential buyer, he would list the Flint RA office number. That way, he could ensure someone would be there to answer the phone.

Because I was the most junior agent, I was expected to answer the phone, transfer calls, and take messages, so most of the old-timer agents would just ignore the ringing office phone. Anticipating the next call would be a big bank robbery or kidnapping and yearning to take on my post-academy career with enthusiasm, I'd answer the phone with "FBI," only to be greeted by someone who wanted to know if the used washing machine was still for sale.

Incidentally, using the FBI office phone number for personal business, like advertising in the want ads, is technically against the rules, but the more senior agents couldn't have cared less. They just wanted first dibs on anything for sale in which they were interested.

An Acronym By Any Other Name Is Still An Acronym

There are literally hundreds of acronyms used in the FBI. The problem is that the acronyms are often duplicative—they have multiple meanings. If placed in the wrong hands, the use of acronyms could be problematic.

CP means one thing when you're investigating child pornography. It means a totally different thing when you're working cyber cases (computer program). When you use an acronym in the FBI, you must think about the context in which it's being used. I often thought we should incorporate the Chinese language, which uses intonation. This would allow the speaker to say the same word but at a different pitch, which would give the word different meanings. I imagined agents running through FBI office hallways, sing-songing their words as they discussed serious case matters.

Federal Bureau of Investigation is FBI. Special Agent is SA. Special Weapons and Tactics is SWAT. Special Agent in Charge is SAC. Assistant Special Agent in Charge is ASAC.

When I worked in Phoenix, I had the good fortune—or so I thought—to supervise the Civil Rights squad for a period of time. What could be more important than fighting the battle to ensure civil rights are preserved and protected for everyone? What could be more rewarding than standing up against ignorance, allowing individual liberty to be embraced?

Occasionally, not realizing some people's dignity had to be protected from my own agents' (albeit unintended) attacks, I had to wonder which side of the battle I was on.

In one case, two of my relatively junior agents were tasked with conducting interviews regarding a crime that may have been committed as an act of racism. FBI agents are the front line of ensuring all persons are treated with dignity—unless, of course, it's the agents themselves who don't realize they are not treating people with dignity.

This case involved an African-America man whose property had been vandalized. The FBI was sent in to determine the reason for the crime, and who was responsible for it. As part of the investigation, the agents interviewed people from the neighborhood, many of whom were African-American males—or, as they're referred to in the government vernacular of information gathering, *Black Males*. Just as the government doesn't care that my roots are grounded in the specific part of Europe known as Italy, I'm only viewed governmentally as a *White Male*. Hence, if their ancestors originated from anywhere on the continent of Africa, in government speak such persons are defined as *Black Males* or *Black Females*.

Why write the same words repeatedly when you can make an acronym with the added benefit of distorting the meaning? As a White Male, I might be identified in writing as a WM. And so the sensitive civil rights agents, charged with a serious investigation to uphold human dignity, unilaterally elected that, throughout their reports, all Black Males would hereafter be referred to as BMs. (Take a moment to consider what BM usually means when someone tells you they had one).

As I reviewed their reports, I found numerous gems of personal information, such as:

"In the course of my investigation, I was able to elicit a BM that had previously not wished to comply."

"Initially, I assumed there would only be one BM, but was able to produce a second," and sadly, for the same agent above: "No BM was produced on this day."

"A BM came forward, which provided unexpected developments previously not released."

"I was able to convince one BM to cooperate with me."

And so on throughout the reports. My agents were having all sorts of interesting BMs at all turns. Clearly, they were determined to get to the bottom of this investigation, and would not allow any sort of blockage to prevent them from ensuring all information was flushed out until the victim was properly relieved. Shortly thereafter, I banned any further use of BM as an acronym.

Elevator Speech

Over the past sixty years, the FBI has played a prominent role in the enforcement of civil rights laws and holds those persons who attempt to obstruct the civil rights of others accountable. While great progress has been made toward ensuring equality for all, one agent inadvertently almost managed to set the entire process back.

As he waited for the elevator in Detroit's Patrick V. McNamara federal building, the agent struggled with an armload of case evidence in boxes piled high over his head. When the elevator arrived and the doors opened, the agent peered through a small space below his boxes, which otherwise blocked his view. All he could see were two legs covered by a long dress, presumably that of the female in the front center of the elevator. The lady just stood there and didn't move.

After a few seconds, the agent became frustrated that she had not moved or allowed him onto the elevator. He finally exclaimed, "Hey, lady, would you move to the back of the elevator?"

She promptly complied, but she chose to move sideways rather than backward. With his heavy load of boxes, the agent entered the elevator and then turned to face the closing doors. As he did so, he saw the elderly woman who'd been blocking the elevator entrance standing next to him. It was none other than civil rights icon Rosa Parks.

Appliance Violence

There are unwritten rules in the FBI.

Unwritten FBI Rule No. 1: Don't embarrass the Bureau. There are many things in the FBI that will get you in trouble, but embarrassing the Bureau can get you fired.

Unwritten FBI Rule No. 2: If you're going to do something stupid, make sure nobody finds out. During a single night in Las Vegas, one agent broke both rules.

While attending one of the many in-service training conferences, an agent had a little too much to drink after hours. Wandering alone through the side streets of Vegas late at night, this agent found himself in the back alley of a casino.

It was here that he came face-to-face with an unexpected adversary. Though larger than the agent, the agent wasn't scared. As a trained FBI agent, he'd looked upon danger before. He knew how to handle himself and had done so in the past; he would do so again. To even the odds, the agent carried on his hip his trustworthy Sig Sauer 9mm 16-shot pistol, which he was well-prepared to use.

His adversary was a kitchen refrigerator. And the entire episode was captured on surveillance cameras.

While I was not present (thank God) for the investigation, I had the good fortune to obtain and view the security video footage. As the brave agent passed the refrigerator, he stopped suddenly in his tracks, took a few steps back, and squared off to face the appliance.

They would do this one on one. Man to machine. Mano a machino. Maybe the agent thought the refrigerator had said something. Maybe it did say something. Who's to say? The internet is certainly changing how we interact with our appliances. Who knows? Based on how the refrigerator had operated in the past, maybe it had it coming.

"Frost-free my ass," I imagined the agent thought. "I'll show you!" Whereupon, as the surveillance video clearly revealed, the agent drew his service-issued weapon and proceeded to empty his gun into the refrigerator.

After surveying his handiwork, the agent holstered his weapon and went on his way. All of this could have been just well and good. No one needed to have ever found out. Upon waking the next day to what was undoubtedly a severe hangover, the agent may not have even remembered.

Alas, this was not to be. Las Vegas is the land of many surveillance cameras, as many as there are glowing lights on the busy strip. That, along with the untrue fantasy of "What happens in Vegas stays in Vegas", it wasn't long before police reviewed the surveillance video and encountered FBI Unwritten Rule No. 2: If you're going to do something stupid, make sure nobody finds out. What they saw was a clean-cut individual draw his gun from a holster. This was no criminal, but rather obviously someone who carried a gun for a living. They put two and two together. Criminals don't use holsters. Only law enforcement wear holsters.

From there, it was just a matter of seeing if any law enforcement groups were in town for a conference and showing photographs of the culprit so he could be properly identified. Hence, violation of Rule No. 1: Don't embarrass the Bureau. Within twenty-four hours, this agent went from attending in-service training to out-processing from government service.

The refrigerator never recovered from its injuries and later had to be replaced at government expense.

A Quick Exit

Lest I appear infallible, here is another example of one of my own blunders: One night while attending an in-service training of my own, I dined in an upscale Middle Eastern restaurant just outside of Washington, DC, with two other agents. We were off duty and the weather was warm, so we'd dressed casually in shorts and polo shirts. This left no place to conceal our guns. In instances such as this, I carried my gun in a fanny pack specially designed to hold a weapon. Should it be needed, a zipper could be opened quickly, allowing immediate access to the weapon. Rather than wear the fanny pack, I'd slung it over the back of my chair. This way, it was not strapped uncomfortably around my waist or hanging off my shoulder while sitting for dinner. It remained close by and within easy reach. Besides, I think we can all agree that few things are as uncool as wearing a fanny pack.

As we attended to our dinner's main course, gravity forced the weight of my gun against the fanny pack zipper holding the weapon inside. This would not normally be a problem, except my fanny pack had been in use for so many years that the zipper had become worn and did not always remain closed. The zipper gave way.

The gun fell out of the fanny pack and crashed onto the restaurant's tiled floor. To make matters worse, the gun slid away from the table and came to rest in the center of the dining area.

If you remember the 1970s and 1980s E.F. Hutton commercial that featured the phrase "When E.F. Hutton talks, people listen," in which everyone in a crowded restaurant would suddenly stop talking when a young professional mentioned his broker was E.F. Hutton, then you know how quiet it got. Everybody in the restaurant came to a standstill. There wasn't a sound. No movement by any of the patrons. Everyone stared at the gun in the center of the floor. Then they looked at me.

I once again refer you to Unwritten FBI Rule No. 1: Never embarrass the Bureau, as well as Unwritten FBI Rule No. 2: If you're going to do something stupid, make sure nobody finds out.

There are numerous government agencies in DC, and many of their personnel regularly carry guns. So, in a situation such as this, there was really only one thing for me to do. I needed to be mature and accept responsibility, which is why I stood up to face the crowd of restaurant patrons, and in my most authoritative voice, announced, "It's all right, everybody. I'm with the Secret Service."

I figured someone would call the police and tell them somebody had just dropped a gun on the floor of a restaurant. To avoid breaking Rule No. 1 and Rule No. 2, my plan was to be long gone before the police arrived. The other agents and I hadn't even touched our entrees, but I threw enough cash on the table to cover the check and the tip while bidding everyone a good night. If the cops did show up after I left, they'd likely call the local Secret Service office and ask if one of their agents had been careless with their weapon in public. It was a brilliant plan.

As I hastily exited the restaurant, the manager turned to me and said, "You may be with the Secret Service, but it's not much of a secret anymore, is it?" At the very least, the manager validated the plausibility of my cover story.

Sticky Situations

The FBI does a very good job in the pre-employment screening process, weeding out those who have issues with drug and alcohol abuse or who might be mentally unsound. All applicants must undergo a very thorough background investigation, including a polygraph exam. Occasionally, a few with something in their past still slip through the cracks.

Fewer than 1 percent of the 35,000 FBI employees ever get into trouble during their careers. For the unfortunate 1 percent, the FBI dispatches the Internal Investigations Division (much like Internal Affairs for the police), which investigates these issues. When proper cause is shown, the appropriate punishment is meted out. This can be anything up to and including termination.

There is also the occasional employee who's not very good at their job, but (remember, this is the federal government) it's very hard, if not impossible, to ever fire anyone. What's left are people with more than personality quirks, like the aforementioned Bunny Boiler—who was, according to her, incapable of being wrong. "I'm always right, you're always wrong" was her motto. They caused me headaches when I was a supervisor. They were the problem employees. I often said, "ISIS is fine. It's my own employees who might kill me someday."

There was once a male agent who sat alone at his desk in a remote three-agent resident agency he shared with two female agents. He was quite content there, working at his computer. That is, until the agents returned and interrupted him in the middle of…masturbating. Now, everyone deserves a break now and then, but this sort of activity at one's desk, in a shared workspace, is generally frowned upon. The agent was subsequently transferred to another division for loss of effectiveness, as it would be difficult for anyone in the division to work with him or take him seriously in the future. Or shake his hand. Or use his keyboard.

I had the same issue with another non-agent employee. While out driving a Bucar, he stopped in a Walmart parking lot for a little personal time. Unbeknownst to him, Walmart security spared no expense when it came to video cameras in its parking lot, which allowed them not only to record the action, but to zoom in for a close-up. So, Walmart contacted the police, who identified the occupant and called me, his supervisor. After viewing the video evidence at Walmart, I removed the employee from any role that would give him access to a Bucar ever again. For good measure, I had the Bucar professionally detailed (in consideration of the future employee to whom it would be assigned). I should have bought the young agent replacing the agent in the previous case a new keyboard as well.

Call Of The Jihad

After 9/11, a tremendous amount of pressure was put on agents to make inroads within the various Middle Eastern communities, and not just to develop information that might lead to potential terrorist plots within these groups. (By the way, terrorism is not limited to Middle Eastern communities; there is plenty wherever you look.) Part of this pressure revolved around the need to better serve the people we were charged with protecting.

When someone from one of these communities decides to step forward, it's important to make sure they're welcomed appropriately.

Consider the well-respected Middle Eastern gentleman with an established relationship in business dealings at the local FBI office. When he decided to be of further assistance, my expectation was that the agent assigned to be his handler would go above and beyond to make him feel respected and at ease. Once seated at the Bureau with his potential Middle Eastern informant, however, this agent decided to play a ringtone he'd downloaded to his cellphone: a chant screaming in a high-pitched voice, "Ahlalalalala … Infidel, oh, infidel. Allah is calling. Infidel, answer the phone."

This was not exactly the first impression I was hoping the Bureau would make with our new informant.

Fired Up

I once supervised an agent whom I ultimately had to fire. The sad part is that this agent should probably not have been hired in the first place. Despite having made it through the FBI selection process, trained, and retrained, she was not tactically sound. She didn't have the ability to make good, logical judgments.

I gave the agent every chance to recover from her lack of common sense, bad decisions, and scarcity of necessary tactical abilities by providing her with additional help and training. She was going to get herself killed, if not someone else. She once showed up at an arrest situation and said to the other agents, "Does anybody have an extra magazine of ammunition they can loan me so I can load my gun?" As a rule, bringing ammunition with you to an arrest is always a good idea when you're an FBI agent.

In another instance, I supervised a non-agent support employee who'd been involved in a road rage incident. I needed to discuss the matter with the employee so I could prepare written documentation of the incident.

"I'm not going to give a statement," she told me, "because I'm going to resign from the Bureau anyway."

"You're welcome to resign if you wish, but as long as you're working here, I need a statement."

"It would be a waste of time, because I'm leaving."

"Before you leave, I need the statement."

No response. "If you don't give me the statement," I said, "I'm going to have to fire you."

"You can't fire me."

"You are leaving me no choice."

"I dare you to try and fire me."

"Oh, yeah? I just did."

Another time, I had to fire an employee who'd been on perpetual leave at home and had refused our request to return to work or provide a doctor's explanation as to why she couldn't. Before confronting her, I found one of the biggest muscular agents I could and told him, "If something goes bad and she gets really upset, I don't have to outrun her. I'll just hide behind you."

However, her termination was no problem at all. She knew it was coming. It turned out she just wanted to see how long she could milk the system and get paid for not working.

Employee Sling Blade

A support employee at FBI headquarters was a less articulate version of Billy Bob Thornton's simple and mentally challenged character in the movie *Sling Blade*. Because he had started saying and doing some wacky things that were very concerning, he became so nicknamed.

One time, I was talking with other agents about how Sling Blade had brought a weapon to work. He wasn't an agent, and federal law prohibits non-law enforcement personnel from bringing personally owned guns into a federal workplace. As I was explaining to the agents that Sling Blade shouldn't do that again, he approached us, picked up a letter opener from the corner of a desk, interrupted us, then looked at me and said, "I don't need a weapon. I could kill somebody with just this."

I realized it was time for this employee to be let go. Otherwise, I feared that someday I might have to use my gun on him.

Awkward Naked Guy

Coincidentally, Sling Blade had a friend I used to refer to as the Awkward Naked Guy. I gave him this moniker because after I'd finished my workout at the FBI gym and was getting ready to head back to my office, this guy would usually corner me in the locker room when he was getting ready to work out or having just come from the shower and wanted to talk business of some sort—totally naked.

Apparently, the Awkward Naked Guy was very comfortable with his body image. I'd be seated on the locker room bench, tying my shoelaces, and he'd walk up to me with towel in hand (but otherwise totally naked) and stop when my head was about to his waist level. "Boss, I have been meaning to talk with you."

One time while I tied my shoes, he put his foot on the bench and began to stretch, leaning slowly in toward his bent knee and bringing the rest of his naked body ever closer to my direction. I'm not entirely sure what he talked about. As you can imagine, I was uncomfortably distracted and not really listening. All these years later, I still cannot unsee certain things.

"Special" Agent Olympics

As a cyber supervisor, I had an entire squad of cyber agents at my disposal. Brilliant with technology, these agents were nonetheless a very different breed of individuals who prided themselves on being highly independent. For a supervisor, it was like herding cats, especially when it came to getting the cyber squad agents to do anything as a group that didn't involve work.

I once offered to take the entire squad to an afternoon baseball game. This meant playing hooky from work. My treat. No one was interested. A few asked if they could go home instead, presumably to play Nintendo.

Around this time, the FBI decided the organization was going to re-emphasize the importance of their agents' physical fitness. When I first joined the FBI and all through academy training, there was an emphasis on maintaining proper physical conditioning. Agents in the field were expected to pass a fitness test twice a year. This meant a timed two-mile run, pushups, sit-ups, etc. Most of us took it very seriously, though the occasional salty older agent would walk the two miles instead of run. While wearing a suit. And smoking a cigarette.

Several years into my FBI career, the biannual physical fitness tests ceased because someone somewhere filed a lawsuit alleging discrimination, possibly because they didn't like to perspire. For whatever reason, a moratorium on the physical fitness tests was put into place, which wasn't rescinded until years later. After the lawyers sorted everything out, and with the FBI then getting back into the physical fitness game, field divisions were given the opportunity to develop their own methods of inspiring their agents to achieve peak physical conditioning.

In an effort to motivate the squads to get physical, someone decided to hold the FBI Phoenix Division Olympics. Each squad would come up with its own event in which all the other squads would have to compete. The idea was to make it fun and challenging. Squad bragging rights definitely played a role. As the cyber squad supervisor, I was at a disadvantage right away.

My agents were hired because they grew up sitting in front of computer screens and had grown into adulthood still sitting in front of computer screens. While some of my agents were very physically fit, only a few of them could be described as athletic. I'm not even sure some of them could be exposed to direct sunlight.

During the creation of the cyber squad event for the FBI Olympics, I lobbied with my squad for an online gaming event but was denied. In the end, I should have expected that the best I could hope for was a relay race using an asthma inhaler instead of a baton.

Call It A Tie

Because most counterfeiting crimes today are perpetrated via the internet, cyber agents work all sorts of intellectual property cases. A number of these cases include those fake emails you receive purporting to sell discounted Viagra. Pfizer, Inc. (the maker of Viagra) once thanked me for my investigative efforts by sending me a nice yellow necktie with its small blue Viagra tablets arranged in a paisley pattern. The tablets didn't say Viagra on them, so no one would know what the pills were unless they'd used them.

I wore the tie to an all supervisor meeting one day. As I sat at a large, fully seated table, another FBI supervisor leaned over and said to me, "Aren't those Viagra tablets on your tie?" From the looks on the faces of those seated around me, it was apparent he had inadvertently revealed that he knew this from experience.

Pregnant Pause

I once attended a training conference in San Diego with several of my agents. We were in the hotel restaurant, seated around a large table and having breakfast. One of my agents, who was very religious, had brought along his wife, who was very pregnant. While the rest of us worked, she planned to vacation in "America's Finest City."

Now when I say religious, I mean their faith was important to them, but not in a zealous, proselytizing sort of way. They bowed their heads and prayed, and then we all ate breakfast.

The wife talked about having their first child. She expressed some concerns about making ends meet financially after the baby arrived. She wasn't certain she'd want to return to work right away. She wished she could find some sort of job where she didn't have to go into an office and could set her own hours. Without missing a beat, one of the cyber agents at the table offered, "Well, you could always work as a prostitute." While this attempt at humor was bad enough, throw in the fact that the agent and pregnant wife were very religious, and it made for quite an awkward moment.

Meanwhile, this type of thing occurred with the same agent a number of times. Sometime later, he and I attended a meeting with a very powerful business executive, a prominent and quite well-known person in the community. I was comfortable in the meeting, but perhaps a bit overly formal because I was in this executive's presence. My cyber agent, on the other hand? Not so much.

The meeting took place the day before Thanksgiving. Meeting in his office, we observed that the businessman had a cellophane-wrapped apple pie sitting on his desk, waiting to be taken home for the holiday.

My cyber agent, in a clear quest to make conversation, blurted out, "Hey, did you ever see the movie *American Pie*? Do you remember the scene where one of the characters decided to simulate sex with an apple pie and unzipped his pants . . ."

I cut him off. "No. Stop talking. Just stop."

Lest you think most agents are like this, remember this is the extreme. There are plenty of good, solid and—yes—*normal* agents who make up the vast majority of the FBI. We also have agents who are the opposite of geeky. We have the cool, suave agents. Being an FBI agent is often considered cool and sexy to those on the outside. Throw in a particularly good-looking agent who can also be charming and you've got it made with the members of the opposite sex.

One such agent resembled a cross between Antonio Banderas and Vinnie Barbarino from *Welcome Back, Kotter*. He was that cool sort of agent who was the envy of others. When out socializing, he always had a beautiful woman on his arm. It was rarely the same woman each time.

When he was on my squad, I referred to him as the Vagina Whisperer. He was amazing, both to me and to the other cyber squad agents, because no one could quite put their finger on what exactly was the element of charm he possessed to attract women. Whatever it was, he had it.

Other agents also thought they possessed these skills, but sadly, they did not. This often ended badly and with negative consequences, for the power of the Vagina Whisperer is mighty and should not be toyed with by mere mortals.

One such agent, thinking himself imbued with this power, took an assignment at FBI headquarters in DC while leaving his family in Dallas. Under the guise of not disrupting family life, he opted to be the good husband and father and report alone, leaving his wife and children behind, returning to visit them on the weekend every four to six weeks.

Now and then, this sort of living arrangement is managed by agents who want to allow their children to finish their studies in the same school and with the same friends, thereby avoiding extra disruption. Our Wannabe Vagina Whisperer (WVW), however, would soon find a girlfriend in DC, and they eventually bought a home together and moved in. His wife and kids would be none the wiser because they were back in Dallas.

After several years, WVW was promoted again. This time, he took a supervisor position in Houston, but decided not to tell his wife and kids in Dallas, leading them to believe he was still working in DC. Meanwhile, he continued to come home every four to five weeks for the weekend to visit his family on a somewhat regular basis. He pretended to have just flown in, rather than the truth of the matter, which was that he'd driven from six hours away and ditched his car at the airport (where he'd pick it up for his return drive to Houston). On top of this, he'd take every opportunity he could find to visit DC on official business so he could spend time at home with his girlfriend.

Sadly, our WVW flew too close to the sun. His wife decided to surprise him one day with a visit to the office in DC. Our ground-breaking almost-polygamist, however, was in Houston at the time. A DC receptionist summoned the DC girlfriend and told her that her boyfriend had a visitor. You can guess the rest.

Our former WVW was soon paying alimony and driving six hours from Houston to Dallas for child visitation. He rarely returned to the greater DC area.

Shoot, I Did It Again

The FBI spends an enormous amount of time on firearms training. From the very beginning of an agent's career at the academy, until their weapon is turned in upon retirement, safety around weapons is always stressed.

Still, being in the FBI is a dangerous business, and accidents happen. Occasionally, those accidents include someone mistakenly firing off a round. This is otherwise known as an accidental discharge (not to be confused with the story I shared earlier about the agent caught masturbating at his desk). Even more rare is when the person responsible for the accidental discharge happens to hit a target—namely, themselves.

Accidental discharges usually happen because the person handling the gun isn't properly focused and has their finger on the trigger when they're not ready to fire. It's happened when holstering a weapon, when moving a gun from one location to another, or even when the person pulled the trigger on purpose, thinking the gun was unloaded. It's a rare occurrence, but it has happened.

For a short time early in my career, I was assigned to work with a task force officer from one of the local police departments. He had the reputation of having had not one, but four accidental discharges, including two in which he shot himself—once in the leg and another time in his backside. Both occasions occurred while he attempted to holster his weapon.

So, when I'd been sent to assist this task force officer with an upcoming raid and we were ready to enter a subject's house with our guns drawn, I turned to him and said politely, "After you."

He probably thought I was being deferential to his seniority, but I just wanted to make sure I was behind him so he couldn't accidentally shoot me as well.

Because of the high cost of living, assigning FBI agents to New York City has always been a challenge for the Bureau. Most agents can't afford to live there on a government salary. It's one thing if you're recruited into the FBI and you're used to living in New York, but it's quite another if you're from a quieter rural area and have to adjust your family to the more frenetic pace and expense of NYC. Some agents assigned to New York end up living as far away as Pennsylvania and have to commute two hours each way to work every day.

One such agent was less than happy to be assigned to New York. Sitting in his Bucar, stuck in traffic, he had time to think about how much he disliked his assigned location of NYC.

He would later explain to internal investigators that, while sitting in traffic, he mindlessly began to toy with an FBI-authorized revolver. With the gun still in his holster, he'd cock it and then gently release the hammer. He did this three or four times. The fifth time, he released the hammer a little too quickly and discharged a round. It went right through the bottom of his holster, continued through the car seat and the vehicle floorboard, and into the street beneath his Bucar. You could literally look through the seat to the roadway below.

This was unacceptable to the FBI. To ensure future firearms safety, discipline was in order. I don't know who made the decision, but someone at headquarters decided the appropriate punishment would be a disciplinary transfer. The agent and his family were uprooted from his New York office assignment and sent to the FBI division in Tampa, Florida.

Word quickly got around the NYC office. Oddly enough, the day after the agent's transfer, that executive decision resulted in five other New York agents having "accidental" discharges inside their Bureau vehicles.

Regarding transfers, there was another unhappy New York agent who, on the occasion of his twentieth anniversary in the FBI, happened to be visiting at FBIHQ that day. The FBI gives employees special pins, otherwise referred to as a "service key," to honor certain anniversaries. Knowing he would be at FBIHQ at this time, the agent had made contact with the director's office in advance so the director himself could present the service key to the agent while having his photo taken for posterity.

After the very brief ceremony, the agent was exiting the director's outer office when he discovered he did not have his new key on him and must have dropped it prior to leaving. Returning to the director's office and apologizing for the interruption, the agent quickly explained he must have left his key behind. After an unsuccessful search, the director told the agent to go to the human resources office and request a new key, scribbling for him on the director's personal stationary a handwritten note stating, "give this man what he wants."

Minutes later, the agent arrived at the entrance to human resources, where he should have turned in one direction to visit the Awards and Recognition Unit for his replacement key. Instead, thinking he would never have another such opportunity again, the agent turned in another direction and proceeded directly to the Transfer Unit, whereupon he approached a supervisor and stated he would like an immediate transfer to the field office of his choice. After being told he was crazy, the agent produced the note from the director. My understanding was that his ruse was never discovered and he lived happily ever after.

Transferring from one city to another can be a regular part of the agent life, but any agent who goes into management will have to spend a few years working at FBI headquarters in Washington, DC.

I worked with one agent who was single at the time. He accepted a transfer to headquarters and found a place in DC, where he settled into a nice rental property in the northwest corner of the city. For those of you not familiar with DC, the city is divided into three sections: northwest, northeast and southeast. There used to be a southwest section, but Virginia demanded it back. Anyway, addresses overlap, so it's always important to look for the city section designation to know where to go. If there's a 123 Main St. NW, that means there is a 123 Main St. NE.

The agent who took the Washington, DC, transfer had been at work for a few weeks, essentially living out of a suitcase, when it occurred to him that the movers should have surely delivered his personal belongings by then. On a work break, he called the moving company and inquired about his possessions. They told him his belongings had been delivered some time ago. The agent protested. He assured the moving company that he was still without any

7

furniture and most of his clothing. The moving company assured him by telling him the address to which they delivered his belongings. The address was correct, but the section was wrong. It should have been northwest, but they took his items to the northeast.

After work, the agent drove over to the northeast address, a considerably poorer community. He knocked on the front door and was greeted by an older gentleman—who was wearing one of the agent's shirts. And pants. And shoes.

The agent poked his head inside the front door and noted the house appeared to be furnished with the agent's furniture. The old man must have thought it was his lucky day when a moving van showed up and started to unload boxes. The agent requested the return of a few personal items, but otherwise let the home dweller keep everything, opting instead to file a legal claim against the moving company.

Years later this same agent had married, and the couple adopted an infant. Sometime later, the agent wanted to rescue a cat from the pound—that otherwise was going to be put down. After completing the application, which detailed where the cat would be living, those in charge of animal adoption told the agent that, unfortunately, he was not deemed suitable to adopt a cat. Apparently, those at the pet adoption agency decided rescuing a cat requires more expertise than raising an adopted child and the cat was better off being euthanized than residing with the agent.

Greater Heights

I've enjoyed some very prestigious moments in my career. I've presented twice at the Vatican, explaining how cyber technology can be used to track people who commit crimes online, and met with the Pope personally on both occasions. I've given talks at other impressive places as well, but not all of my moments in the FBI have been stellar performances.

We've all found ourselves in awkward situations of our own making. It happens to all human beings from time to time. Who among us hasn't found ourselves accidentally creating a circumstance that could prevent our fellow coworkers from passing a required drug test, right?

I had a sister-in-law who was a bit of a free spirit. She was all about peace, love, and harmony. She was kind, but could be naive. And she liked to bake.

During one of her visits to my home, she baked a bunch of Twinkie-size banana breads and wrapped them individually in cellophane. In fairness, they were delicious, but I really didn't need all those extra carbs lying around my house. Being the kind and generous person I was, I brought the mini banana breads to the FBI office for my coworkers to enjoy.

You probably realize by now that agents will eat anything brought into the workplace if it's free. As a result, most of those banana breads disappeared as quickly as they arrived. I then put the remaining breads into a large basket and placed them in the squad area on top of a filing cabinet, where people could help themselves.

Later that night, I arrived home after work and was asked by my former outlaw—I mean, in-law—if I'd eaten all the banana breads. I assured her that while they were delicious, I'd shared most of them with others at the FBI office. She expressed great relief and said she didn't want me to eat too many at one time because she'd baked them with her secret ingredient—hemp.

For the uninformed, hemp is used to make a lot of products, like rope and clothing, but it contains the same active ingredient that causes marijuana users to get high—THC. Unlike marijuana, you'd have to consume an awful lot of hemp to get high, but if you were drug tested, the results appear the same.

Upon learning this news, I recalled my profession was one that regularly engaged in random drug testing and I was struck with fear. If a random drug test were performed when I arrived back at work, I'd fail. This would put my job in jeopardy, not to mention that anyone who consumed the banana bread could be subjected to random drug testing as well. Unless I could prove I'd been contaminated through no fault of my own, the situation didn't look good.

Without another word, I ran from the house, jumped into my Bucar, and—just shy of using the lights and siren—raced back to the office.

Once there, I hurried to the squad area. It was after-hours by then, so all of the agents were gone. Unfortunately, so was most of the banana bread. On the desks of various agents, I found a couple of uneaten banana breads still wrapped in cellophane. Regrettably, I also found quite a few cellophane wrappers in the trash cans. Thanks to my sister-in-law, I'd just succeeded in getting my entire squad technically high.

Every agent on the squad had eaten at least one banana bread. Some, many more. For every one of us, a random drug test was a real possibility. There was only one thing I could do. Play the odds: Say nothing.

The THC from the hemp would pass through the bloodstream in days or weeks, anyway. So rather than incur the wrath of my coworkers, I kept the secret to myself. I figured if anyone was called in for a drug test, I'd come clean. Fortunately, time went by without a single drug test for anyone on the squad, though there was one agent who came to work the next morning and told everyone he couldn't believe how many bags of Doritos he'd eaten the night before. In time, I decided it would be a good and proper thing for me to own up to the other agents about what happened.

I'll do that now. If we were on the same squad in 1998 and you're reading this now, you have my sincere apology for any inadvertent apathy or weight gain I may have caused you.

Special Storage

Though not an agent, this story about the single mom/FBI employee is well worth including, as I think you'll agree. She got by on low pay and was the sole support for her son, a typical college kid who could be a little irresponsible. Such was the case when he'd left a padlock on a storage locker his mom had rented temporarily for him, which resulted in her getting billed for two additional months. She called to apologize to the storage facility for her son's mistake, but they wouldn't budge on the charges.

"My son is special," the mom explained.

"All our kids are special to us," the storage employee said.

"No. I mean, my son is *special*," she said, intentionally implying that her son was mentally challenged—which was actually not the case.

"Oh, I'm sorry. I misunderstood," the employee said. "As soon as the lock is removed, we'll be happy to reverse the charges."

Soon thereafter, the FBI employee sent her son to the storage facility to remove the lock. When he returned home, he told his mom, "The people at the storage facility were nice, but they treated me strangely, talking slowly and using small words. They even offered me a cookie."

Practical Jokes

In the world of agents, and law enforcement in general, practical jokes are a common occurrence. Sometimes they're innocent, such as putting confetti in the air conditioning vents of an agent's Bucar, so when the agent turns on the A/C, they're showered with a thousand tiny pieces of paper. Or they can be more sinister, like replacing the confetti with pepper spray, inflicting greater, albeit temporary, damage to the agent.

All agents learn to never leave their computers unattended. A practical joker could create a false email and confess some made up dark secret to fellow squad mates. An email might just as easily lead to something more problematic, like if it's sent to the director of the FBI demanding a transfer to one of the Bureau's less desirable locations. Humorous or not, practical jokes generally remain in-house. Unless, that is, you happen to be like one unlucky agent.

When an agent mistakenly left his computer unattended, his squad mate seized the opportunity to enter the lonely computer and access the agent's FBI Microsoft Word software, where she thought it would be funny to auto-replace every occurrence of the agent's name with the phrase Loser Boy.

A little background about an FBI report is in order. An agent's name can appear in a report multiple times, including at the bottom of the first page where the agent signs their name. Instead of FBI Special Agent John Smith, the report would now read FBI Special Agent Loser Boy.

The joker's intention was to surprise the agent, who would, of course, catch the error, and everyone would have a good laugh. Unfortunately, the agent who wrote his report didn't bother to proofread his work closely enough. Not only did he not notice that his name had been replaced with the Loser Boy moniker, he even signed his name at the bottom of the report to confirm it was complete.

No worries, though. Upon completion, all FBI reports are turned over to an agent's direct supervisor for scrutiny and approval. However, in this case, his supervisor didn't feel the need to read the report too closely (maybe because he thought the agent was such a stellar performer), so he signed his initials right next to the agent's signature directly above Special Agent Loser Boy, officially signing off on the report.

The report then made its way to the permanent FBI file, where it was photocopied and provided to the prosecutor for review in preparation for an upcoming trial.

As expected of any good prosecutor, the report was again copied and provided to the arrested subject's defense attorney. After all, shouldn't his client enjoy the constitutional right to see all the evidence that would be used to prosecute him, including the names of the agents in pursuit of justice?

The time came for hearings before the judge in advance of trial, and the defense submitted a request to cross-examine Special Agent Loser Boy. Yes, the defense just copied the name from the FBI report. Now, it either had to be admitted to the defense attorney that FBI agents had been playing practical jokes on one another, or somewhere in the Bureau we would have to find an agent who's actual name was Loser Boy. Not being able to provide the latter, we did the former. Hence, another violation of the "Don't embarrass the FBI" rule.

At the time, I was the FBI assistant special agent in charge of the Phoenix office. I summoned the practical joke-playing agent to my office for her appropriate disciplinary reprimand about her unprofessional behavior. Fortunately for the agent, the whole situation was so funny that I couldn't keep a straight face, so I just told her to be sure and never to do it again.

AND AS SUCH IS CHARGED WITH THE DUTY OF INVESTIGATING VIOLATIONS OF THE LAWS OF THE UNITED STATES, COLLECTING EVIDENCE IN CASES IN WHICH THE UNITED STATES IS OR MAY BE A PARTY IN INTEREST, AND PERFORMING OTHER DUTIES IMPOSED BY LAW.

Office of the Director
Federal Bureau of Investigation

BY ORDER OF:
The Attorney General
of the United States

Having left my credentials unattended, a practical joker replaced my official FBI identification photo with a picture of Liberace. For about two weeks I introduced myself to numerous members of the public by displaying my credentials before noticing the prank.

The Supervisors

The FBI, like most professional organizations, takes great pride in its leaders. If FBI agents are supposed to be the best law enforcement has to offer, then logically, the FBI leadership should represent the best of the best.

Solid leadership should inspire confidence and be conducted with humility. A leader should be tough, but kind. A good leader should listen to employees and have enough emotional intelligence to hear what's not being said as well as what is.

I'm proud to say that many FBI supervisors possess these qualities (and more), making them the superior leaders they are.

As you've likely guessed by now, this chapter is not about those FBI leaders and supervisors, but the rest of them. Despite the lack of many (if not all) of the characteristics previously mentioned in a good leader, these few somehow managed to rise to a position of authority within the Bureau.

SAC Attack

Every employee in the FBI office is required to wear an identification badge known as a Security Access Card, or SAC badge.

(This is not to be confused with the SAC that stands for Special Agent in Charge. Again, with the acronyms!) The badge is used for more than physical identification. It's embedded with a chip that allows for computerized entry into the FBI building and its various levels when the card is waved in front of an electronic reader. Without a SAC badge, an employee is unable to get through any door in the building, let alone into the building itself.

When I first arrived in San Diego as an FBI agent, the machine that makes the identification badges was broken, so I was without a SAC badge. Because my arrival to the city coincided with another agent's departure (under orders to transfer out of San Diego to another assignment), my supervisor believed he'd devised the perfect solution and instructed me to just wear the SAC badge of the now departed agent—a genius idea except for the fact that I was a white male and the departing agent was an African-American female. Nevertheless, the embedded chip in the SAC badge would get me into and around the FBI building. I wore the badge for three weeks, until the machine was repaired and my own SAC badge was produced.

The funny thing about this tale is this: Even though I was new to the office and few people there knew me, for the three weeks I wore the African-American female SAC's badge, not once was I stopped or challenged. Maybe it was a better idea than I gave my supervisor credit for at the time.

Getting In His Licks

As I have previously stated on several prior occasions, the vast majority of agents were solid people and performers, but there was always the odd one who was able to slip through the screening process and be hired. And these few agents are the bane of existence for those who have to supervise them.

A supervisor friend of mine was working in the transfer unit when he was made aware of another headquarters agent who had gotten himself in trouble and was to receive a disciplinary transfer, demoting this individual out of headquarters and back to being a street agent, along with the loss of both authority and pay that goes with such a demotion. This agent's transgression? Apparently he licked another employee.

Neither I nor my supervisor friend ever became aware of the exact circumstances surrounding the licking in question. Dogs will often lick persons they like and it can be assumed this agent was engaging in similar behavior, as he had apparently approached a co-worker of the opposite sex and licked her on the face. Had she possessed a rolled up newspaper, the agent might have received punishment of a swat across the nose and told *down boy*, but instead the employee properly reported the incident to her supervisor. As part of the demotion, the agent would normally be transferred to the nearby Washington field office, just a few blocks away from headquarters. However, my supervisor friend in charge of transfers was waiting on a transfer himself to the very same location. In an effort to ingratiate himself with his future boss by not bringing him a potential problem employee, my friend instead thought he would cleverly transfer the licking agent instead to the Detroit Division.

Several years went by and my friend, having forgotten all about the licker, found himself now in Detroit as the head of the office. In the middle of one night he was awoken with a call from a Detroit FBI supervisor stating that an agent had engaged in inappropriate conduct aboard an airplane and had been arrested. It appears the licker agent was traveling on a late night flight, and eyeing a woman seated alone across the aisle from him, leaned over and licked her face. Unfortunately, for this agent, the woman, who was startled awake, was married to a special forces soldier who had been in the plane's lavatory. When the husband returned to his seat and heard from his wife what had occurred, he proceeded to lick the agent's face, only the solider husband used his fists instead of his tongue.

Beaten thoroughly for his lingual advance, the agent's problems had only just begun, as upon landing he was placed under arrest for assault on the female passenger. Regardless of this agent's legal problems, it would inevitably mean problems for the boss in the form of bad publicity.

My supervisor friend had managed to avoid having to deal with this agent for years, but yet could not escape the inevitable, and ultimately had the licking agent dismissed from the Bureau's service. His whereabouts are now unknown, but I like to think he found a future working for a 31 Flavors.

Where The Web Is Going

When dealing with FBI headquarters in 1995, I often found a lack of forward-looking vision. Back then, computers were becoming so commonplace in everyday life that it was clear to me cyber technology was going to change the way crime would be committed in the future.

"Cybercrime" wasn't a word being used yet, but I tried to be ahead of the game, and as I was a young agent at the time, I hadn't yet had the enthusiasm for my job beaten out of me. So, being somewhat computer-savvy, I wrote a proposal to FBI headquarters explaining how I thought the internet could be used to fight crime.

I explained how the FBI could develop its own website, which could feature fugitives' photographs and profiles and give the public a way of reporting information online.

For my efforts, the FBI rewarded me with a rejection letter in which I was basically patted on the head kindly and it was explained to me, "While the internet has proved a popular forum for entertainment and some businesses, its utility for law enforcement purposes is not readily apparent at this time."

In consolation for my attempt to help the FBI become computer-savvy, the Bureau did enclose a nice FBI pen and pad of stationery. My twenty-first century solution had been met with a nineteenth century attitude.

Supervisor John I.

In my own role as supervisor, I did my best to keep things light and inject levity whenever I felt I could; in one case, my squad prepared to execute a search warrant on the residence of a subject who'd been identified as having stolen wedding photos of actors Tom Cruise and Katie Holmes. At the time of their marriage, they'd made a business arrangement with *People* magazine, giving it exclusive rights to publish their wedding photos. The theft of those photos breached the contract, which was said to be worth millions of dollars.

This certainly wasn't as important as most cases the FBI works, but our search of the subject's residence was likely to receive a lot of media attention because of the celebrity victims. For this reason, I wanted a few extra agents to assist the squad.

In a call for volunteers, I circulated a Tom Cruise-themed email:

> "As the squad supervisor, I am looking for *A Few Good Men* and women to participate in the execution

of a search warrant which some thought was *Mission: Impossible*. Because there is some *Risky Business* involved, I will need my *Top Gun*. To stay safe, we will need to make *All the Right Moves*. Those assigned to other squads may participate as a *Collateral* duty, so please do not think of yourselves as *The Outsiders*. Yes, I would like agents from *Far and Away* to be involved. The weather is expected to be without *Rain; Man* and woman will remain dry as there should not be any *Days of Thunder*. We will be seizing, among other things, green, as in *The Color of Money*. The Firm date has been set for this search warrant, and I will be assigning someone to conduct the *Interview With the Vampire* who committed this crime. When we are done, we can all enjoy a nice *Cocktail.*"

Humor Positioning

"You're not what I was expecting for an FBI agent." I've heard that many times in my career, being contrary to the stoic television image of how an FBI agent should act.

I was once in a very serious meeting at FBI headquarters with the FBI director and other high-ranking officials. A senior officer from London's Scotland Yard was sharing some of the security issues it was having dealing with "today's world of terrorism" at its very large football venues. "By the way," I interrupted. "I'm here as the official English interpreter. When he says 'football,' what he means is 'soccer.'" Although it wasn't the funniest thing I'd ever said, everyone laughed. If you use humor successfully, it's interesting how it positions you.

I've often attended meetings where a colleague would attempt to be funny, sometimes at my expense, even in a good-natured sort of way (though sometimes not), and regardless of whether their comments fell flat or not, I was already well-prepared to launch my return volley comment.

Comedy, like a Bureau-issued handgun, can be a dangerous weapon when it's not in the hands of a properly skilled individual. It can make you look foolish. But if you're good at it, you stand out even more. I've been to plenty of supervisor meetings where people couldn't remember a thing that was said, but they remembered a funny comment I made. While that may seem meaningless, the truth is you can elevate yourself to the lead position in the right circumstances if your comment is remembered in a positive way.

Of course, there were inappropriate times to use humor. I never used humor while prepping for a SWAT operation. SWAT is serious business. You wouldn't want an agent involved in a shooting investigation to reveal later he didn't catch everything that was said because "John was telling jokes."

All the same, with just a few well-chosen words, I could take the forefront of leadership by capturing the audience's attention at the right time. I've walked onstage at conferences and had my introduction met with barely a smattering of applause. But break away from the expected serious persona of an FBI agent and open with a funny comment or joke, and the audience will sit up and listen. Even if the material being discussed is serious, technical, or not particularly exciting, if humor is incorporated, the audience will hang on every word, anticipating the next laugh-worthy statement.

Except when part of the audience doesn't want humor, like during Super Bowl XLII, when someone hacked into a Tucson,

Arizona, cable television company and interrupted the halftime show with a three-minute excerpt from a gay porn movie. Needless to say, exposing pornographic images to those watching the game—including many young children—is a criminal offense, so the FBI opened a case. When FBI headquarters in Washington, DC, took an interest in this high-profile hacking, a videoconference was held with the FBI field office, of which I was a participant. During the conference, referring to the length of time the program interruption lasted, an FBIHQ executive asked how long it was.

"About six inches," I answered instinctively. The field office burst into laughter, but the Washington executives did not seem amused.

Verbal Judo

Inside and outside of the FBI, I've found no matter what business you're in, there will always be competitors who won't necessarily wish you well. Humor can be the great equalizer. More than once over the years, I've referred to several adversarial colleagues by stating, "I would not engage him in a battle of wits any more than I would engage an unarmed man in a gunfight. And for the same reason."

I've always considered it high praise when someone decided to take a verbal jab at me in front of others, only to be warned by a colleague, "Ooh, you don't know who you're messing with here. I wouldn't do that if I were you." The tip of the hat to my being quick-witted was not lost on me.

I sometimes used humor to put people in their place, but I always reserved it for those who were most deserving of it.

There was one extremely arrogant supervisor in Phoenix who frequently spoke down to others. At an all-supervisors meeting, he once said he'd not met many people in the office because he was relatively new to the division. In an attempt to neutralize some of his abrasiveness, I remarked, "You will find two types of people in this office: those who don't like you and those who haven't met you yet."

Message delivered: Rein in your behavior.

As a supervisor, it wasn't all about dealing with case issues. There were matters I never considered when I entered into management, but someone has to make the decisions, and many of the issues that crossed my path could be unusual.

The AO

In the FBI, the AO is the administrative officer, who's basically in charge of all aspects of the physical office and its functioning, including evidence control and the evidence room.

My squad had just completed a complex investigation involving the sale of used airplane parts that were being illegally represented and sold as new. This was a serious public safety issue. As such, we'd seized a large quantity of physical evidence stripped from out-of-service planes, including various components ranging from cockpit computer circuit boards to large airplane propellers.

Our large and complex search had been planned well in advance. During the planning period, I'd coordinated with the AO, as we'd need a place to store the trial evidence. From the beginning, the AO seemed uninterested (in general and in particular) with assisting agents in the matter. Even though this was the exact type of function the AO was paid to perform, it was almost as if our need for space to store the evidence was a nuisance and caused him unnecessary work. In reality, he needed to do nothing more than find a large storage facility the government could rent and install an alarm system to prevent anyone from accessing the area undetected.

After a long, physically grueling day (have you ever picked up a rotor blade from a helicopter?), we returned to the office at 5 p.m. Our timing was perfect. The AO was just leaving his office for the day and heading toward his specially assigned parking space.

"Where did you arrange for us to secure our evidence?" I asked.

"I've not gotten around to it."

I was shocked, to put it mildly. "What am I supposed to do with a box truck full of airplane parts?"

"I don't care," he said, apparently annoyed that I was keeping him from being out of the parking lot by 5:01 p.m. "It's not my problem. It's your evidence. You figure it out."

He got in his car and drove off. *Fair enough*, I thought.

I decided to take what the AO said literally. I'd find my own place to store the evidence. I instructed my agents to unload the box truck and stack everything in the AO's personal parking space. The parking was covered, and the lot was surrounded by a fence. In addition, a twenty-four-hour guard was on duty. *How much safer could the evidence be?*

The next morning, I got to work extra early. I was in my office when I heard the AO stomping his feet, yelling furiously about what I'd done and heading my way. He arrived yelling at me, but got no satisfaction and marched off to the office of the special agent in charge to plead his case, which fell on deaf ears.

I was commended by the SAC for my resourcefulness. Only then was the AO properly motivated. Before the day was over, he'd located a place in the FBI building where our evidence could be held, which also guaranteed he'd have a place to park the next day.

For a while, the story became legendary in the office, and the AO suffered much embarrassment. Eventually, he angered the wrong person with his poor attitude and was given what the Bureau refers to as a *loss of effectiveness* transfer and sent to another office to begin anew.

Survivor: The FBI Edition

The FBI has some of the greatest leaders in law enforcement nationally, and for that matter, anywhere in the world. The hallmark of a good leader is to inspire your people, put their needs in front of your own, and lead by example. The skills necessary to become an FBI agent represent these attributes of leadership. With trial by fire, numerous agents evolve even further, enabling them to lead other fine agents through the challenges of fighting crime.

On the other hand, there are always those select few who were promoted for one reason or another, often to the detriment of those who must follow. Generally, FBI agents are defined as the type of individuals who are brave and willing to put themselves on the line, be it by risking physical danger or standing up for those unable to protect themselves from injustice. The inability to make a supervisory decision is not part of this definition.

A squad in New York City had one agent more than permitted. This meant someone from the squad would have to be reassigned to a different, understaffed squad. The supervisor of the overstaffed squad couldn't decide who should be transferred. Maybe he didn't want to become unpopular with the agent he might select and was afraid to do so. Regardless, someone was going to leave the squad and would probably be unhappy about it, as would the other agents in the squad who liked working with the agent being transferred.

And so, in a moment that can only be considered such a terrible idea that the uniqueness of it must have made it seem brilliant to the squad supervisor at the time, he decided the decision as to which agent would be selected to leave would be made by the squad agents themselves. The supervisor declared the entire squad would enact a "tribal council," as in the television show *Survivor*.

The supervisor then called the entire squad together into a conference room and held the tribal council, sans torches. The squad supervisor instructed each agent to cast a secret vote for the agent they wanted off the squad. After this was completed, the supervisor channeled his inner Jeff Probst (the host of *Survivor*), and after the votes were tallied, for dramatic effect, read the name of each voted-off person to the entire squad, one at a time.

The vote was very close. In the end, a female agent was asked to extinguish her virtual torch, informed her tribal squad had spoken, and asked to take her leave.

The fearful supervisor had achieved his goal and removed an agent without having to make a decision. Yet in this creative and exuberant effort, he also created chaos, as those who received votes from other agents of this once tightknit squad now wanted to know who'd voted for their reassignment.

The female agent voted off the squad later found redemption. Not on an island like on *Survivor*, but in the form of a lawsuit she filed against the Bureau for the purposeful humiliation she'd experienced, otherwise known in the legal world as the intentional infliction of emotional distress. She didn't quite win the $1 million *Survivor* prize, but was awarded a large settlement.

Out Of Sight; Out Of Time

For two weeks, I was out of the Phoenix office to attend to Bureau business that an assistant special agent in charge (ASAC) had ordered assigned to me. Meanwhile, during my work absence, my cyber agents worked a case using very sophisticated new technology.

A criminal subject was going online and committing cybercrimes, but from different locations each time using different Wi-Fi connections. This made it very difficult to track him down. The speed at which he moved from one Wi-Fi connection to another led us to believe he was operating his computer equipment from his car.

My brilliant cyber agents developed a method to track the subject while he was online and to do so in real time. The problem was that, while technology had advanced, the law hadn't necessarily kept pace. To obtain a search warrant for the subject, the address of where we were going to execute it had to be specific. This allowed the subject to move to the next Wi-Fi location before a judge could sign a warrant with the correct address and before agents could execute the search.

The ASAC was very frustrated by this. He also didn't really understand the complexities of what the squad was doing and thought my agents were disorganized and—because I was out of town rather than on location—not receiving the proper leadership they needed to obtain the warrant.

It took quite a while, but the subject finally remained in one place long enough for a search warrant to be obtained, for the agents to detain him at the identified location, and for the vehicle to be searched for evidence.

I returned to the office from my assigned Bureau business after all of this occurred and was promptly summoned to the ASAC's office. Despite the success of the search warrant and the squad's use of new, highly sophisticated technology to locate the subject, the ASAC still perceived things as having not gone smoothly and that I was to blame as had not been present for the operation. I tried to explain to him the technical complexities he clearly wasn't grasping so he could be assured that things actually went very well. I also reminded him the only reason I wasn't present for the operation was because he'd sent me away on a two-week assignment.

Despite the facts, he refused to concede. "A failure of leadership occurred because you were not in the office," he told me.

I'd learned not to fight battles in the FBI just because you're right, and to let it go if it doesn't matter in the end. As this was the case, I figured I'd let the ASAC continue to believe whatever he wished.

I excused myself and was just walking out the door when he called me back in. "John, before you go. You did a good job on the two-week assignment I sent you away on. In appreciation, I am giving you a time-off award."

I'd just been reprimanded by the ASAC for not being at work because he had sent me away, and in the very same conversation, he gave me a reward of more days away from work. Another great example of government leadership in action.

And They Called It Puppy Love

The FBI thoroughly examines each prospective candidate, including a background check and polygraph exam. All types of people apply to work for the FBI. Many of them are great candidates. Some are not so great. Some you might even consider odd—or worse.

I've had people applying for a job with the FBI confess to crimes while undergoing the polygraph examination. It's very kind of these people to turn themselves in (rather than make us investigate a crime and then have to go pick them up), but as thoughtful as they may have been with their confessions, committing a crime precludes you from FBI employment.

Unfortunately, as the supervisor, there were other behaviors the office polygraph examiner reported to me. To this day, I've been forced to carry around those mental images, the memories of which I've been unable to erase from my mind's eye.

On one such occasion, the FBI considered hiring a promising female candidate. Her résumé was outstanding, and by all appearances, she'd add to the level of FBI excellence it strove to maintain. Only the pre-employment polygraph examination stood between this woman and her quest for Bureau employment.

The polygraph examination contained no specific questions regarding animal ownership, but the examiner said he detected some issue of evasion with the woman. Being a professional, my polygraph examiner probed a little deeper, dogged in his pursuit of the truth. When I saw the examiner later, I asked how the exam went. He simply replied, "Too much puppy love."

I had absolutely no idea what he was talking about. *Was she stalking an old flame? Was she a pet hoarder in violation of the health code? What?*

The polygraph examiner explained that she had admitted to a crime: an act of bestiality where she'd allowed puppies to perform oral sex on her. An otherwise promising candidate dismissed from consideration. Doggone it.

Supervisor Silencer

When I worked on the street gangs task force, I had a supervisor who believed a clean desk was a sign that an agent didn't have enough work to do. Because his desk was a mess and mine tended to be neat and orderly, this became an area of contention. To get him to stop questioning how much work I was doing, I created a collage out of a desk calendar. I glued all kinds of papers and other assorted desk items to it: Post-it notes, paper clips, etc.

Thereafter, I maintained an orderly desk when I was working, but whenever I left the office, I took the collage out of my drawer and placed it on top of my desk. Every time the supervisor saw the collage, he assumed I was fully immersed in the proper amount of work. He never bothered me again.

After a few days off from work, I returned to my supervisor job only to find my office furniture had been removed.

That Which Cannot Be Unwritten

There is a saying in the FBI: "If it is not written down, it never happened." From day one, agents learn the importance of documenting every aspect of their work. Every single thing an agent does is documented. An agent meets with a source (i.e., informant); there is a report. An agent interviews a witness; there is a report. A soon-to-be-dismissed director meets with the president who is eventually going to fire him (whether or not he believes it is his personal notes); there is a report.

In regard to written documentation, this is one of many areas in which the FBI is extremely thorough. On the other hand, there may be such a thing as too much documentation.

The Most Interesting FBI Agent In The World

It had been a full day, and I'd just returned to the office to check emails and work on my reports. There's a certain methodology to writing an FBI report in a way prescribed by the FBI. In many ways, FBI agents are like scientists. When an agent prepares a report, it's very fact-based. There's no room for literary flourishes and definitely no place for opinions. Agents only report the facts and allow others, like judges and juries, to draw a logical conclusion.

Yet one report widely deviated from the norm. It was filed by a special agent whom I will henceforth refer to with the fictional name Bart Langdon.

We've all done things to embarrass ourselves somewhere along the way in life. FBI agents are no exception. Goodness knows, I'm certainly lumped into that category. Some agents, like Bart Langdon, go to great lengths to embarrass themselves. This guy was a relatively new special agent at the time.

The report he wrote concerned his participation in the investigation of a kidnapping and the subsequent rescue of a young child. Blatantly ignoring the FBI rule of facts only, Langdon's report made gratuitous use of phrases intended only for dramatic effect. For example: "I knew we had to act now!" What investigative relevance does that have? None.

Bart Langdon was very proud of his report writing. Unfortunately, when he shared his report with one of his academy instructors, he exposed himself to the condemnation of his peers. After reading Langdon's report, the academy instructors surely thought, *Oh, my God. What did he do here?* The instructor sent it to a colleague. That colleague sent it to others, and they sent it to others. That kind of enthusiastic sharing happens a lot in the FBI. Next thing you know, Bart Langdon's report had made its way clear around the Federal Bureau of Investigation until virtually everyone had read his travails.

As it circulated throughout the FBI, I, too, was an email recipient of Langdon's report. Agents are great about sharing stuff like this, but to make matters even better, while the emails moved throughout the Bureau, agents added their own comments to the email thread before they shared it. You know the routine. You receive an email with the subject line stating, "You have to read this." You open the message, scroll to the very bottom to read the original message, and then work your way toward the top as you read the superfluous commentary.

In a moment, I'll share with you a short sample of Bart Langdon's original FBI report, otherwise referred to within the Bureau as an FD-302. The original is quite long, so I've removed all but the pieces that tell the primary story. I've left just enough to give you a sense of Langdon's, uh, writing. I've also removed agent and law enforcement personnel names to protect the innocent. Remember, this is supposed to be a report consisting of 100 percent facts and nothing else. Bart Langdon became infamous in the FBI because of this report, which read like a cheap detective novel:

> I felt a distinct awareness, based upon a combination of experience and training, that backup could take a fairly long time to arrive on the scene, that each second would count, and that the victim had a small chance of survival if we did not take action as the officers on the scene.-

> I then proceeded up the stairs and attempted to kick in the door. After a few tries, it was obvious that it would not breach without mechanical assistance or many more kicks.-

> The victim seemed to instinctively know we were there to help and smiled at me.

We—the other agents in the Bureau and myself—*had* to add commentary to his original email, because what Langdon wrote is *not* how you write an FD-302. Some agents opined in their best imitation of the Dos Equis beer commercials about Bart Langdon, "the most interesting man in the world," or in the theme of Chuck Norris jokes as "the toughest man alive." All these agents started chiming in on this email commentary about how pretentious this guy was when he wrote about his FBI work:

> Did the FBI director hear how Bart Langdon turned a glass of water into orange juice by waving a magic wand?
>
> Everyone knows kidnapped children love magic.
>
> As Bart Langdon thought of himself, a small smile crept across his face . . .
>
> Chapo, Nacho, and the Zetas are no match for Bart Langdon, "Master Magician."
>
> I glanced down, making sure no doughnut crumbs or flakes of white sugary frosting were clinging to or crusting my Brooks Brothers blazer.
>
> Chuck Norris, "Texas Ranger," would never have crumbs of doughnuts on him, and neither would Bart Langdon, despite the earlier low crawl at the Krispy Kreme.
>
> I felt a distinct awareness, based upon a combination of experience and training, that the Texas Rangers could not accomplish such a low crawl with a hot, tasty treat in one hand and a volcanically hot cup of coffee in the other.

Did I smell a hint of mischief in the air, or did I sense the special agent in charge might be getting slightly vexed from my daydreaming like a schoolgirl?

Just like Chuck Norris, one day people will say that "Bart Langdon's tears can cure cancer; too bad Bart Langdon never cries," or "Bart Langdon is so fast that he can run around the world and punch himself in the back of the head," or "Bart Langdon counted to infinity twice," or "Bart Langdon let Kenny G live; Bart Langdon doesn't kill women," or "Behind Bart Langdon's beard is not a chin, but another fist" and "Superman owns a pair of Bart Langdon pajamas."

Disinfect This Email

The following email thread is a fine example of what happens when you hit "send" without thinking about how others will respond. The first email is real and was sent by a supervisor. This made him a legend of sorts. The reply is priceless.

----Original Supervisor Message----

From:	**(redacted) (FBI LA)**
Sent:	**Thursday, June 08, 2006 11:29 AM**
Subject:	**Disinfectant non-response**

No one has contacted me to let me know if they were going to pick up the disinfectant in supply and take it to the fitness center. If someone has, please email me now, and disregard the rest of this message.

If no one has picked it up, someone needs to. Just so you all know, when I ask for help, it is only because I really need it. I am the SSA (Special Agent Supervisor) of a squad of 19, and I am in the process of standing up a task force which is going to wage war on some really good criminals in the Glendale area who are stealing hundreds of millions of dollars from Medicare every year. On top of that, I have asked and been authorized by the assistant director to remain the office's point guy (as I have been for the past three years) on the new building project, the cost of which will likely exceed $1 billion dollars by completion.

Right now, we are in the middle of a political firestorm as we try to gain funding to build. We have already been funded $17 million for design, but we are balancing on a knife edge right now as we attempt to gain congressional approval for construction funding over some very effective local opposition.

More importantly, I try to be a good husband and father every day by attempting to work only ten hours a day, but I often fail there and work beyond that. So, while I had time to do the emails necessary to buy the disinfectant, now I need some help getting it from the supply room to the fitness center.

I am not unloading on anyone. I know you are all good and dedicated people and you all had the initiative to volunteer to help. I am, however, reminded of a case some twenty years ago in New York City in which a person was mugged and brutally beaten to death in an alley as some forty residents in their apartments looked on from above. None of them called the police. In subsequent interviews, when asked why they did not call for help, each said, 'I presumed someone else would.'

Thanks,

----End of Supervisor Message----

Here now is the reply that made famous both the original email and the agent who responded.

----Agent Reply----

Reply From: **(FBI LA, address redacted)**

Sent: **Thursday, June 08, 2006 5:42 PM**

Subject: **RE: disinfectant**

In many ways, the author and I are kindred souls in search of cleansing. He, through the time-honored ritual of physical pain designed to end with elevation above the mortal realm through the spiritual fire that is *disinfectant*. And I, through the little-known but similarly effective rituals of self-mutilation and race-baiting.

And when I heard, much to my dismay, that no person from this esteemed list had contacted him to say that they had picked up the disinfectant, I cried out in anguish and in shame: "I am bleeding, I am bleeding, but the fighter still remains . . ." Or maybe that was Simon & Garfunkel.

But regardless of little things like copyright infringement and the current instability in the Middle East, we must all band together on this issue of cleanliness, or we shall all certainly fall to the slovenly gods that now reign supreme in the gym. And you know whom I'm referring to . . . that balding, middle-aged male wearing the shirt just a little too tight with the stain on the front that speaks of unnatural acts with mustard and relish in days gone by, or the female with the come-hither stare and the belly that protrudes ever so slightly over the spandex pants.

Yes, we all know these people, and we all know that only scalding by disinfectant can cure our gym of this infestation.

And a man with a squad of 19, a father of wonderful children, a builder of buildings, a developer of task forces and wager of war against the sinners of Medicare in that den of iniquity, Glendale, California, cannot be expected to do it himself. He needs help from those people who would otherwise visit New York as tourists and watch a man get beaten to death in an alley, probably as part of a "snuff" film, without calling the authorities. He needs help from you and from me, and from the homeless vagrants who make their home in the bushes off the Santa Monica exit. He needs us all.

Some of us he needs to help pick up disinfectant. Others he needs to help when he counts to one billion, and let me tell you, with enough zeros, you could try to count to infinity when those zeros are placed behind any number from 1–9. Still others he needs to look after his children and wife when he works beyond a ten-hour day. And for those of you who perform that particular duty, we will need yet more people to look after your children and wives and husbands as you go beyond your ten hours.

As you can see, the cycle is never-ending. A butterfly flaps its diaphanous wings somewhere in Malaysia, which creates a breeze that blows all the way to southern Lebanon. That breeze washes over the face of Hassan Nasrallah, who decides that, as leader of Hezbollah, the breeze is a sign from Allah ("There is no God but God and Mohammed is his messenger") that he should have his group kidnap two Israeli soldiers from the northern Israeli/Lebanon border, which in turn causes Israel to unleash hell on Lebanon, forcing most of the leaders of the G-8 summit to condemn the Israeli response as too draconian, which Israel promptly ignores as it hits yet another Beirut power station, causing the price of oil to rise to yet another high per barrel of $78, leading to an even greater shortage in the fuel budget of the Los Angeles Office, causing the assistant director in charge to park cars to save money so that the person scheduled to pick up the disinfectant has to travel on foot in a bad neighborhood, and we can all see where that leads.

Like our author, I'm not unloading on any one person. Just those with initiative and volunteers in particular. Especially the so-called "good people."

So, let's get the lead out and help our author save his soul through disinfectant.

----End of Agent Reply----

Mass Emails

One of the unique things about working for the FBI is that, despite the position you hold in the organization, we are all equals in many ways. The lowest common denominator of this equality is that any one person in the organization is equally capable of writing an email message and sending it out to the entire office. There are those who've sent their manifestos to the entire FBI worldwide for all to read, bringing shame just as often as fame upon their heads.

Here then are just a few of the literary gems for which the "send'" button should never have been clicked.

Personnel assigned to FBI Headquarters received the following email:

"Today's wellness class has been canceled due to illness of the instructor."

On the heels of that email came one that originated from an FBI agent in a field office who accidentally shot himself in the hand while at the range. Few of us knew about the event until this email arrived in our inboxes:

"Sir, I wanted to thank you for maintaining confidentiality in what happened yesterday so as to not cause me any more embarrassment than I already feel."

And the reply?

"Well, son, if you wanted to have kept it confidential, you should have sent your email to me rather than the entire Bureau, which is what you appear to have done."

This one is from a support employee who apparently skipped English in any of his school years:

"Hello, If anyone needs a five foot by five foot freight box on pallet there is one in the loading dock. It also have ton of bubble wraps in it. If no one needs it or wants it. It shall be disposed on Friday."

And a short time later, this email from the same sender arrived in my inbox:

"Box have been Claimed. Sorry."

Five Good Men

The following are real messages posted via email and are provided here verbatim for your reading pleasure. Here is a motivational gem:

> Gentlemen, if someone asks you to move a SWAT vehicle—**you will not**, as those are assigned spots and that is where the vehicles go. If you see someone dicking with my vehicles, then please notify me so that I can express my concerns and fears to them over a cup of Folgers International coffee, and I can make them feel better about themselves and let them know that their kung fu is no good.

Last but not least—I will be gone quite a bit through the end of the year. I am hoping that when I get back, you have looked deep inside your souls to see if you really want to be on the SWAT team. I have been here lots and lots of years and intend on being here lots and lots more years. As the XO of this group, I take it as my responsibility to oversee what you do while the CO deals with all the front office issues. Having said that, I feel it is my utmost duty to let you know that some of you have made this collateral duty quite the pain in the ass.

I take full responsibility for what I consider a lackluster effort that you put forth. Many of you have issues—including lack of motivation, no initiative, no drive, no team, no esprit de corps. Many of you have a lot of "What about me?" attitudes which I really don't care for. SWAT isn't about having cool gear, standing around like you're a stud, lady killer, etc., 'cuz you ain't. Many of you like to throw your kit on like you stormed the beaches of Normandy, but in reality, most of you haven't been on more than a few ops, so your level of expertise is equivalent to, well, actually nothing. Additionally, none of you have no grounds to tell anyone how to solve a tactical problem. A little humility and a shut mouth go a long way. A few things to consider so that I don't have to consider them for you:

1. You will never, ever, ever use SWAT as an excuse for not doing something you're supposed to be doing (investigations/file reviews). I will be letting your supervisor know to fill me in when you do.

2. You are not as good as you think you are—none of us are.

3. You will self-motivate or I will assist you with that motivation as I kick your ass out the back door.

4. Q: Do I step up and help out? A: No. But I am gonna fix that because I want to be part of the team.

5. Q: Why am I a shitbird?

6. It is a privilege to be on SWAT, not a right.

If you need to ask yourself, "Is he talking about me?" then you probably should ask yourself that again. If you think that maybe there is no way that I could be talking about you, then you probably are part of the problem.

We have a lot of yuks and laughs, but this isn't the Las Vegas joke team; it is the Las Vegas SWAT team. Wednesday, 0800, black shorts, tan PT shirts and running shoes—back parking lot by ET garage. Rain, sleet, snow . . . all your gear for inventory laid out. We will then have motivational PT afterward, and you will be on my schedule. Gents, I'm not here to win a popularity contest, I am here to provide the division a tactical team, and that I will. In the infamous words of SA (redacted), 'Give me five good men...' If you have issues with any of this, come see me.

Here are some of the responses from other agents to this leader's email, which were then forwarded around the Bureau world:

"So grows my chapter on motivational supervision."

"Now this is how you lead people."

"File this in the ever-growing 'this can't be real' file."

"Oh, boy..."

"Sir, it is the private's duty to inform the drill instructor that Private Pyle has a weapon and is locked and loaded."

"Wow, somebody really loves themselves a lot and is severely under-assigned."

"Wow, I am motivated to turn my gear in."

"I like the way this man thinks. I believe we should implement some of these steps immediately. Especially the motivational PT. 'Beatings will continue until morale improves.'"

(More) Ludicrous Emails

I was sent an email concerning a threat made against the Super Bowl. Because the Super Bowl is considered a high-profile priority, we suspend normal investigative operations and cover these types of leads immediately:

Subject: preliminary analysis of email address ********@yahoo.com

Sent: Monday, January 26, 2009 8:00 AM

A nonspecific threat was made against the upcoming Super Bowl game, for which the email address resolves to your jurisdiction, necessitating the sender be contacted and a judgment be rendered regarding the sender's ability to carry out the threat. The email address ********@yahoo.com resolves to a website called Fat Kids of America. The website also listed a Myspace page for Fat Kids of America. A search on Myspace of the same email address revealed a page for "Curt (is a nerd)" with a private profile indicating the subject is 16 years old. Let us know if there is anything else we need to be concerned about. Thank you.

And my response?

From: Iannarelli, John G. (PX) (FBI)

Sent: Monday, January 26, 2009 8:51 AM

And to think that actually, at one time, I dreamed of becoming an FBI agent. Yet my Monday morning now begins with addressing threats from the "Fat Kids of America." Can't we just distract him with a Twinkie until the game is over?

Intelligence Reports

Every interview I ever conducted was documented in writing. Likewise, when interviewing a subject of a crime, another agent was present to serve as a witness. The FBI does this because, when faced with the likelihood of conviction in a later court hearing, most subjects will say anything, often claiming they were threatened and coerced into confessing. Having a second agent present helps with corroboration of what the subject said.

One time, the subject of an embezzlement investigation confessed her crime to me. I let her leave the office and drive her car home. I knew she wasn't going anywhere, and after completing all of the investigative work I arrested her a few weeks later.

She claimed in court that I threatened to arrest her and take her children away if she didn't confess to a crime for which she now claimed to be innocent, although the stolen money she deposited into her personal bank account indicated otherwise. On cross-examination, the defense implied she'd been threatened. I explained I had no intention of arresting the subject on the day of her confession, no matter what she said. Gratuitously, I added: "She could have confessed to the Lindbergh kidnapping and I was still not going to arrest her that day."

Little did I know that, post-conviction, the subject's attorney would appeal and use my quote in the official record. There's nothing terrible about that in and of itself, except that appeals heard by the courts eventually get printed in lawbooks for all the legal world to see. This case was over twenty years ago and I still receive the occasional call from someone who's come across my comments while conducting legal research.

Midget Assassins

This was initially classified as secret, but shortly thereafter declassified. Someone in the Bureau received information from an informant and decided it was important enough for an official intelligence document to be formally prepared and shared—not just in the FBI, but with all other pertinent law enforcement agencies. This was done so everyone would have situational awareness of a serious imminent threat. According to the source, drug cartels were now employing midget assassins.

The term "midget" (not my words; used by the source) was used to indicate subjects who are much shorter in height than the average person—approximately three-feet tall. Allegedly, cartels had elected to employ these midget assassins because "they are able to operate unnoticed." People overlook them—literally.

The report went on to state, "Source believes that employing a midget assassin is actually now considered a status symbol, because not everyone can have a midget."

Why is that? Are they too expensive? Are there not enough midget assassins to go around? Why were these questions not answered by the FBI? What are they hiding?

Apparently, for high-ranking cartel personnel, money is no object. Fortunately, thanks to the intelligence-gathering efforts of the FBI, US law enforcement heightened its alert and focused downward. We were to be on the lookout for this growing, and also non-growing, threat.

I still think there is the distinct possibility someone wrote this as a bad joke, but nevertheless, it slipped through the cracks and was disseminated throughout the FBI and North America's law enforcement agencies.

Pimp Plan

Just like dealing with midget assassins, another intelligence document was prepared to make sure law enforcement officers were properly acquainted with the criminal mindset. In this case, the pimp. While most of the information in the document was common sense (at least as far as the criminal following these guidelines was concerned), I never understood the necessity of sharing this information with the entire law enforcement community.

The intelligence document contained notes written by a pimp and left behind at his residence after he was arrested for operating a prostitution ring. Ponder these gems of business advice, courtesy of the FBI intelligence program:

No. 1: Get more bitches.

No. 2: Keep bitches working.

No. 3: Keep the bitches fly.

No. 4: Every day bitches not be working not be making me money.

Certainly, words everyone in the business world can live by.

The Cases

Everything the FBI does revolves around casework. Because a subject is the one who's suspected of committing a crime, the FBI builds a case so the criminal might be brought to justice. A source shares stories about what the bad guys are doing. A case is opened, and the source is put into operation to gather evidence. In any work the FBI undertakes, there's always a case and a case number for the file the work is associated with.

The necessity of having an open case prevents the government from randomly investigating someone or something just because it feels like it. For a case to be opened, the checks and balances of having an open case require a "reasonable suspicion" of a crime. It's a much lower standard than conviction (beyond a reasonable doubt); it requires a show of criminality beyond mere suspicion, but less than the probable cause needed to make an arrest. Most times, of course, the subjects make it very easy to prove reasonable stupidity.

Cowboys And Indians. And Israelites.

I sat in my ASAC office one Christmas Eve and looked forward to going home early to enjoy the holidays. But an angry rabbi had other ideas.

This rabbi didn't belong to any synagogue. He opened his own place of worship and chose, of all places, an Indian reservation. He got into an argument with his spouse, and sadly, it turned into a domestic violence situation. When the police responded, he held her hostage inside their home on the reservation. Because it was federal land, the FBI had jurisdiction.

Agents, SWAT, hostage negotiators, and others were dispatched to the scene, which was several hours' drive from the office. I arranged for a formal case to be opened. Given the confluence of the impending Christian holiday, the Jewish faith leader, and all this happening on Native American land, I thought a more than general case name would be appropriate, hence, *Operation Mishegoss*. No one else in the Bureau seemed to understand my sense of humor. Some thought it was the name of an Indian tribe. My Jewish readers are probably laughing right now.

Catch Me If You Feel Like It

As an FBI agent in San Diego, I conducted bank robbery investigations regularly. One time, when the robbery had happened a few days prior, I conducted all the follow-up stuff FBI agents do when a bank robbery has occurred. I took witness statements and went over everything with the bank manager to make sure I hadn't missed anything.

As I sat with the manager at her office desk, I went over the details of a statement I'd heard and written practically dozens and dozens of times before. "Give me the money now or I will shoot you." Few bank robbers have any sort of flair for originality.

The assistant manager poked her head in the door and looked at the manager and me. "Excuse me, but somebody is trying to pass a bad check right now at the counter."

Game for any break in the routine of going over witness statements, I followed the assistant manager to the teller counter and approached the guy she was talking about, the one trying to pass the check.

"Hey, can I talk to you for a second?" I showed him my badge and pulled him aside.

I quickly ascertained that yes, he was trying to pass a bad check. As a precaution, I hooked him up with handcuffs, not wanting him to get squirrelly on me. I hadn't searched him yet, so from a law enforcement officer safety standpoint, I knew he could have a weapon. I didn't want to have to shoot him. I certainly didn't want to write up the required paperwork if I did. I was not enjoying writing witness statements as it was, so if it meant not shooting this guy, well, damn it, I'd do whatever it took not to have to put further pen to paper.

More importantly, though, I was wearing a nice suit with no desire to get it dirty. Unlike it was for my police uniforms, dry cleaning was not an FBI agent tax-deductible expense.

How did I know he was trying to pass a bad check? A better question is, how did the bank teller know? This is the story of a local mope.

A *mope* is a law enforcement term for an individual who's likely to be involved in some sort of criminal behavior. It's somewhat above jaywalking, but below the level of organized crime. The term comes from the old violation of mopery, where someone could be charged for loitering where they didn't belong. We just call them aggressive panhandlers today. If you've ever driven a car in New York City, you've probably had your windshield cleaned by a professional mope with a squeegee. Sort of like the Mr. Goodwrench of vagrants.

This mope had been going around stealing outgoing mail from mailboxes attached to homes or at the edge of the sidewalk. It's a very common practice. I tell people: "Never put your outgoing mail in your mailbox for pickup, especially if it contains checks. Take it to the post office." When people put their outgoing mail in their mailbox, they usually put the flag up on the mailbox. The flag is like a signal to the criminal: "Hey, you. Yeah, the one with the crystal meth-pocked skin and that faraway stare in your eye. Come steal my mail."

Every time this mope would find an envelope addressed to a utility company he knew there would be a check in an envelope, and he'd take the check home. The envelope, too. Can't have people knowing their outgoing mail has been stolen.

Once home, he'd apply acetone—a colorless, flammable liquid solvent typically used for cleaning in a laboratory or removing nail polish—to take the ink off the check without ripping or damaging the paper. The acetone just washes the ink right off.

In the mope's case, it's also a convenient additive to increase the volume of his crystal meth concoction, like how Grandma used to add Wonder bread to her stuffing on Thanksgiving.

Contrary to what you might think, a check doesn't always get indented when you write on it with a pen. Many pens don't let the ink sink into the paper. It depends on what kind of ink your pen uses. I recommend people use certain pens because the ink will bleed right into the paper, making it impossible to remove with acetone. The one *not* to use is a ballpoint pen, because that ink can easily be washed away.

After the bank criminal took the ink off the section of the check where the amount was written and to whom it was made out, he rewrote it out to himself and changed it to a larger amount of money. He would be reasonable with the amount he made out for himself because he wouldn't want the check to be rejected by overdrawing the account.

The check in question was from a notable national bank. (I don't want to say which one, but let's say it rhymes with Tank of America.)

He picked a Tank of America branch at random, away from the area where he stole the check. This way, he wouldn't run the risk that one of the tellers would know the holder of the account and become curious as to why a check was written to him. He'd enter the bank, knowing they'd cash a check drawn from one of their branches. He'd pick a time of day when it was busy, because it's always better if there are a lot of people around, as it would be less likely he'd stand out. There might even be other mopes in line waiting to cash their own stolen checks, so he'd blend in.

He got in line. Several tellers were helping people at the counter. Pretty soon, he was called up by the next available teller. He stepped up to the counter and handed his check to a female teller. She took the check. Looked at it. And stopped.

She just stared at the check. It was her check. He'd stolen it from *her* mailbox. She didn't live in the neighborhood where the bank was located. She commuted to her job at the bank. For that matter, just like the mope who stole the check.

What are the odds that someone would steal mail from a random neighborhood, pick an arbitrary bank, get in line, get called up to a teller window by a specific teller who just happened to be available to help the next person in line, and then it's *that* teller's check?

Add to this that there also happened to be an FBI agent in the bank at that very moment, albeit with a nice suit that he desperately wished to remain clean.

So, there I was with my gun and my credentials. I even had my handcuffs. I got to take this guy into custody and get a stat (statistic, like points) for making an arrest. In law enforcement, it's all about the stats. How many arrests? How many reports? How many cases?

And there I was, with one handcuffed stat I got for very little effort.

After transferring my subject to the local police for a ride to jail, I told the agent who accompanied me, "Given the odds of this kind of luck, we're definitely stopping on the way back to the office and buying a lottery ticket."

Who's Your Daddy?

While working on the reactive squad charged with investigating bank robberies, kidnappings, etc., I received an extortion case. According to the credit card company, a new card had been delivered by mail to a woman, but she indicated she never received it. Instead, she'd been a victim of credit card fraud and on top of which had received a threatening letter in the mail related to the theft of her credit card.

Like the story of my previous mope, I suspected someone had stolen the mail from her mailbox. When the woman received a bill for purchases she didn't make, we knew the thief was using her credit card. Before the woman could cancel the credit card, she received a letter that stated if she called the police, canceled the credit card, or did not pay the bills racked up for the unauthorized purchases, she'd be killed by the credit card thief.

While certainly scary, what made this case unusual was that the extortion letter wasn't handwritten or typed, but was prepared by cutting out individual letters from magazines and spelling out the entire message by pasting the letters on a sheet of paper, like what you'd see in an old gangster movie.

Even though someone had committed this crime, you have to appreciate the workmanship involved in preparing the extortion letter. Criminals just don't have the work ethic today they once had. That attention to detail and pride of ownership is gone. Today's thieves are all about type, click, send. But I digress.

My female victim was very distraught, but it didn't take me very long to figure out who might be behind the crime. All the letters appeared to have been cut out of magazines for a teenage audience. Also, the letter had no postage. It had simply been placed in the mailbox. It just so happened that a teenage girl lived right next door to the victim.

One evening, I went to the residence. I hoped to speak with the parents before I talked with the girl. Upon approaching the house, I clearly heard a heated argument going on between the teenage girl and an older woman (whom I presumed was the mother). As bad as the girl was being in the argument, the older woman was worse. She cursed relentlessly and used terrible language directed at the teen. I even heard a couple of slaps. I knocked on the door and announced myself: "FBI."

The argument stopped. Things got quiet. After a minute or two, the girl answered the door. She wasn't intimidated at all by my presence and instead was very hardcore.

"What do you want?"

"I want to speak with the other woman in the house."

"F— off."

"If you don't get the other woman to the door, I'm coming in."

After cursing me out a little more, the teenager eventually got the other woman to the door. She identified herself not as the mother, but as the babysitter, as the teen's father worked nights at a downtown bail bonds business.

As I wasn't getting anywhere with the alleged babysitter or teenage girl, I learned the purported father's name and business location, and then drove over to have a chat with him.

If you've never been inside a bail bonds business, think sleazy adult bookstore but without the ambiance or class. They can be very seedy, with their clientele standing around and waiting.

I explained the reason I was there and about the extortion letter. The father seemed relieved that was the only reason I was present, which I thought was odd. He admitted the teen had probably written the letter and he'd have a chat with her.

I brought up the issue of the babysitter and that I'd overheard abusive behavior toward the girl. To my surprise, the father defended the babysitter, saying the daughter got out of line sometimes and needed to be slapped every so often. That answer was not going to do.

The next morning, I contacted child protective services. After a little research, it turned out things were not as they appeared. The babysitter was actually the teenage girl's mother. (She'd denied being the mother because she had warrants for her arrest and provided a false name at the time of my inquiry).

Without letting on what I'd learned, I called the father and advised him that either he or the babysitter would have to bring the girl to my office to give a statement before I could close the case and not bother them anymore. I advised him that the FBI does not arrest minors, and no matter what they told me, the girl wouldn't be federally arrested.

After I pestered him with calls and multiple visits to his home, the father eventually brought the girl to my office. She confessed to both stealing and using the neighbor's credit card and to writing the threatening letter. Likewise, the "father" finally admitted he was actually not the teen's father, but the "babysitter's" boyfriend, acknowledging she was actually the girl's mother.

As we left my office, I reminded them that the FBI does not arrest minors. No matter what the girl told me, she wouldn't be arrested by anyone from the FBI.

However, when we reached the exit, I introduced the daughter and her mother's boyfriend to a police officer (whom I'd arranged to be present and was able to arrest minors), and he arrested the girl for grand theft and extortion—in lieu of the feds not being able to do so. I then told them the police were at their residence at that very moment arresting the mom for her warrants.

The boyfriend was free to go. Because he was in the business, perhaps he was able to arrange a bail bond discount.

Undercover

After eight years in the field, I was promoted and assigned to Washington, DC, as the FBI's national spokesperson. I like to think it was a competitive process and I'd been selected from the best of the best, but in truth (by now having a better understanding of how the government operated), I knew deep down it was probably a choice between the guy with Tourette's syndrome and myself. The other guy probably passed on the offer.

As I had referenced earlier, Eric Rudolph, the Olympic Park bomber and one of the FBI's ten most wanted fugitives, was captured in 2003. Despite the success of this capture of a high-profile FBI fugitive, made by a keen-eyed North Carolina police officer, one of the FBI assistant directors was very unhappy and called to yell at me.

"Why are you talking to the media about this case?!"

"Haven't you heard? I'm the spokesperson for the FBI. This is what you pay me to do."

Apparently, that was not the correct answer.

Hot Tub Soon To Be Serving Time Machine

I once investigated an insurance fraud case that involved a well-known, wealthy business leader who was regarded as a pillar of his community. However, one of his businesses wasn't doing well financially, so of course, this reputable businessman decided to do the right thing. He'd give his employees two weeks' notice, arrange for severance pay, and liquidate his business assets.

Nah, just kidding. Actually, he decided to burn his business to the ground and collect the insurance money. To my good fortune, the community leader took it upon himself to hire someone else to do the dirty deed for him. That *someone* just happened to be one of my sources, who was all too happy to wear a wire so we could record the businessman soliciting arson and insurance fraud.

The meeting between the businessman and my source went exactly as expected. The community leader/businessman offered to pay my source to throw some gasoline around and burn down the businessman's building. As a bonus, my businessman subject (married for a long time, with children) also solicited my source for sex in exchange for money so he could engage in a homosexual affair.

Now he was on tape soliciting a felony to burn down a building, but the misdemeanor solicitation for prostitution charge would prove to be more problematic—as it would likely require some explaining to his wife.

While all of this went on, unbeknownst to me, another guy who owned a business adjacent to the rich businessman's building also wanted to get rid of his business. He had the very same idea that the way to go about it would be to burn down his building, too! This second guy, however, was a much more hands-on sort of fellow. Imagine a do-it-yourself businessman who cuts out the middleman, along with the homosexual prostitution solicitation. Why hire someone when you can light your own building on fire yourself? So, maybe it burns down my subject's building in the process as well, although arsonist number two did not know arsonist number one had the same goal.

When I first learned a fire had broken out in the building, my immediate reaction was, "The wealthy businessman had hired someone else to start the fire and didn't follow through using my source." Only later in the investigation did I learn what actually happened. Eventually, both subjects were convicted: one businessman for solicitation of arson and the other businessman for the actual arson. Both were also charged and convicted of insurance fraud. The irony is that if the rich businessman had just waited a little while, his neighbor would have burned down the building for him and he could have legitimately collected on the insurance claim.

During my investigation, I also discovered the actual arsonist made a bunch of fraudulent insurance claims for losses to property in the "accidental" fire, including a large jacuzzi that had allegedly been in storage in the building. However, I also learned that prior to setting the fire, the arsonist removed all of his valuable items from the building—including the jacuzzi.

During the post-fire investigation of putting together a case, I went by this second guy's house. His property was surrounded by a tall wooden fence, so I walked through the adjoining neighbor's backyard, climbed the fence, and sat on top of it. What did I see but the arsonist and his girlfriend relaxing together in the supposedly destroyed hot tub! I used my Bureau issued camera and captured the two of them on film in the hot tub post fire. When the case was brought to trial, those photos made excellent exhibit evidence of the insurance fraud.

Speaking Of Fraud

I once arrested a con man for fraud. The law firm he chose to represent him—I swear—was named Spender & Robb.

Would You Like Fries With That?

I'd been assigned an embezzlement case; a bookkeeper had abruptly quit her job at a McDonald's restaurant. She disappeared from her last known residence after it was discovered she'd stolen $50,000 from her former place of employment. The McDonald's was on the grounds of the San Diego Marine Corps Recruit Depot, which was federal property. This made it a federal case, removing investigative authority from Officer Big Mac and turning it over to the FBI. Although $50,000 is a lot of money for the average business owner, in the FBI world, agents generally deal with much larger cases and much bigger numbers.

I had a full caseload at the time—kidnappings, bank robberies, and extortions—cases where actual lives could be at risk, so the bookkeeper would have to wait until I found some spare time in my schedule. The owner of the McDonald's didn't understand this. He thought I wasn't taking his case seriously. He'd been leaving me voicemails telling me he wanted to see some action.

One time, he called my phone and caught me at my desk. He demanded his case become my top priority. I tried to reasonably explain my other cases and the time constraints, but he wasn't having any of it. He continued to press. This went on for a while, until he told me that, as a respected businessman and taxpayer, I needed to remember that I worked for him.

If I worked for him, I was long overdue for a raise, not to mention that someone needed to do something about all of those unpaid hours I was working. As calmly as I could, I told him that, respected businessman or not, I didn't care if he was Mayor McCheese. I was not going to ignore lives that were on the line for his case. I would get to it as soon as I could.

I would have done exactly that, had he then not called my supervisor after hanging up with me. After complaining to my supervisor, the next thing I knew, I was working full-time to solve the embezzlement. Nevertheless, it wasn't a very complicated case.

The bookkeeper handled the money. She marked the books with the money that had been collected. She was supposed to deposit the cash at the bank. The money never got there. There was enough evidence for me to get an arrest warrant, so I just needed to locate the bookkeeper and take her into custody.

The problem was that after the bookkeeper quit her job, she moved from her last known residence without leaving a forwarding address. I knew she had family in the area and she was born and raised in San Diego. Without having any ties elsewhere, I figured it was unlikely she'd fled the area, especially with only $50,000 in stolen cash to live on. She had to be somewhere close to her familiar surroundings.

Fugitives are often caught at the homes of family members because there is a human tendency to remain close to the familiar and comfortable. The question was where to start looking. I tried speaking with her known family members, but either they didn't know where she was residing, or more likely, they didn't want to cooperate with the FBI to have her arrested. Fortunately, I had another avenue of investigation I could pursue.

I failed to mention that this bookkeeper was particularly large. Her driver's license listed her at 5 feet 4 inches and 250 pounds, but I figured based on photographs that she was at least 300 pounds or more. This gave me an idea.

Armed with a photo of the bookkeeper, I went to the area where she'd previously resided. I started visiting all the fast-food restaurants in the area, one by one. Sure enough, after a couple of tries, an employee at a Burger King counter told me, "Yeah, I've seen her before. She comes in every morning for the French toast sticks."

At last, my first solid lead! At 7 a.m. the next day, I stood outside Burger King with another agent. Just as I suspected, my bookkeeper showed up right on schedule for her French toast sticks. We grabbed her before she entered the restaurant—mostly because, if we waited until after she left the restaurant, her hands were likely to be sticky from syrup.

Show Me The Money, Pirate

I responded to a bank robbery with some agents from my squad. The two subjects involved, a man and woman robbery team that was far from professional, had already been spotted and detained by the local police. They were drug addicts in search of cash who hadn't thought through their getaway.

Their escape plan was to be on foot, but this proved problematic as the man only had one leg. In place of his missing appendage, he wore a prosthetic that was, quite literally, a peg. My only experience seeing someone with a peg leg was in pirate movies, never in person. I don't recall any peg-legged pirates walking too quickly, and certainly not running from the police. This peg leg made a clicking noise with every step he took. Had he not been discovered so quickly, we may have been able to continue tracking him by sound.

Despite their inept getaway and quick capture, the robbers didn't seem to have the stolen money on their persons. With police assistance, we retraced the route they traveled (or hobbled), but were unsuccessful in finding the money. Besides hoping to return the stolen money to the bank, getting a conviction is a heck of a lot easier when you can produce evidence of the stolen cash. It was time to convince at least one of them to tell us the truth about the money.

We separated the two subjects, and I talked with my bank pirate in an attempt to find out where he'd hidden the booty plundered from—I kid you not—Seacoast Bank. He denied knowing anything about any money. He continued in this vein for some time. As we stood outside on the concrete sidewalk on an unusually warm San Diego day, me in my Bureau suit, I began to lose my patience.

"I know you're lying," I told the pirate, "simply because I can tell that both you and your story don't have a leg to stand on." Honestly, how many times in life would you ever have the opportunity to use that expression in a literal context?

Eventually, I wore down the subject. He finally said he knew where the money was, but "someone is going to have to retrieve it."

"No problem," I said. "That's what we do. Just tell me where it is and I will personally get it."

My peg-legged pirate subject leaned in close to me, and referring to his partner in crime, whispered, "Have you checked her vagina?"

It took a moment for it to register.

I've found money hidden in a lot of places in my career, but this would be a first. Understandably, I was no longer eager to be the one to go looking for it. Because the money was inside of her, we needed a search warrant unless the subject was willing to give consent. Plus, I'd never done any searches like that before. Would I need my gun? What would I find once I'd, excuse the expression, made entry? Where is the Vagina Whisperer when I need him?

To my surprise, after I told the female bank robber what I knew, she provided consent to be searched. Was her consent a reflex reaction? I found it unlikely she'd say no to anyone interested in having a look down there. Nevertheless, off to the hospital she went, where a trained professional with a signed consent form performed a successful cash-ectomy.

The doctor reported how much cash was removed, and we recorded the amount and denominations. I recall it was quite a bit of money—more than I thought could possibly be hidden there. I asked the doctor if he was certain all the money retrieved was from the bank robbery. As expected, he didn't have any expertise in that sort of thing. In any event, there's a lesson in all of this: don't put money in your mouth; you never know where it's been.

Mr. & Mrs.

I've worked many threat and extortion cases in my career. Some of the subjects have been much more creative than others. In one case, death threats were being made against a husband and wife for the sole purpose of intimidating them. The couple was rightfully concerned. The person making the threats had traveled to their residence, set foot on their property, and left behind an ominous message.

Did he throw a brick through their window? Stick a knife in the front door to hold up a menacing letter? No, this criminal's approach to sending threats was much more imaginative: In the victims' driveway, he placed Mr. and Mrs. Potato Head figures to represent the couple. What's so disturbing about that? Did he stand them up in the driveway with a sinister letter in their hands? No, that would be mere child's play with a child's toy. Rather, he laid them flat on the ground on their potato backs, then chalked a body outline around each potato victim. To emblazon his ghastly intent, he added a potato peeler beside one potato cadaver and a potato masher beside the other.

As odd as it may seem to you and me, it's hard to understand the mindset of someone going to all of the trouble to purchase Mr. and Mrs. Potato Heads, assemble them, and then place them on the victims' property in the precise way he did. The perpetrator turned out to be an angry coworker of the husband and wife. As odd as his MO was, it was probably easier than writing a threatening letter on an Etch-A-Sketch.

Crime scene where the subject had staged Mr. and Mrs. Potato heads in the victims' driveway in an attempt to intimidate them.

The Sources

All agents are expected to develop informants, aka *sources*. The word *informant* often conjures up the image of some dirty criminal from a back alley—someone with no allegiance to his fellow criminals, who would sell them out to get himself out of trouble or in exchange for money. While this is sometimes the case, more often than not, sources are law-abiding citizens who've become aware of someone who's committed a criminal act and want to help their community by providing information to the FBI.

I've operated many sources over the years, almost too numerous to count; some worked in strip clubs or were run-of-the-mill incompetent criminals, while others wore suits and carried briefcases to work every day. Regardless of the type of source, one thing every FBI agent learns is that, to gain their cooperation, you need to build rapport with them. For the source to be productive and successful, he or she needs to believe the agent handler is truly concerned about their well-being.

With the white-collar informant, it was easy, as we had many similarities in life: job, home, and family. When it came to developing rapport with the criminal element, this could be more difficult. On many occasions, you had to avoid passing judgment on the poor decisions they made in their lives, such as hurting innocent people, including their loved ones. Sometimes, however, building rapport was best achieved by maintaining objectivity.

Uncle Sam

In June 2004, documentary filmmaker Michael Moore released his movie *Fahrenheit 9/11*. I was the spokesperson for the FBI's press office at the time, and a quote from yours truly was displayed on the big screen.

I saw the movie. It was awful. It was so bad that, had I been watching it on an airplane, I still would have walked out. I still believe Michael Moore owes me a $10 refund for the ticket price.

Shortly after the film's release, I started getting a lot of emails from fans of the film. They were anti-war, anti-government, and anti-FBI. They emailed me to vent their anger over alleged cover-ups and conspiracies. For a while, I became the focal point of one particular conspiracy theorist who would send me daily rants.

I quickly learned that trying to engage in an open dialogue with someone who also believed the moon landing was faked was probably not the best use of my time. However, as the FBI spokesperson, I couldn't just ignore taxpaying citizens, either. I eventually penned a generic email response that I'd copy and paste to appear as if it were an autoreply. My prefabricated response was specifically designed to appear as an official notification that their message had been received and the FBI was appreciative for their having taken the time to write.

The average expletive-laced emails from these senders would thus be greeted by the following message:

Dear Gentle Reader—Thank you for having taken the time to write. Please excuse this autoreply to your email, but as you can imagine, I receive so many messages each day from people like you who are supportive of the FBI's mission that it would be impossible to reply personally to each and every one. Please know that your kind words mean so much to all of us here at the FBI. Because you have taken the time to write, your message will have specifically caused us to strengthen our resolve and continue doing what we do each and every day. Again, your concern and support for the FBI is an inspiration.

This response would sometimes prompt the original emailer to reply with an even angrier second message, to which I would again copy and paste, "Dear Gentle Reader—Thank you for having taken the time to write. Please excuse this autoreply to your email, but ..." It became my little game.

Of all the emails I received as a result of Moore's movie, there was one person who identified himself only by his first name: Sam. From the time he'd written his first message, it was clear he thought of himself as my personal informant. He immediately began passing me information, and he proved to be a prolific writer who would email me *every single day*—sometimes, multiple times a day. Sam would send me information that was of no investigative value whatsoever. Frequently, I couldn't distinguish what it was that concerned him in the first place and prompted him to write.

Some highlights from Sam's prose:

"Two men seen talking on street corner. Please investigate."

"Stray dog wandering in park may be trained to gather information. Please investigate."

"Items in my home have been stolen and replaced with exact duplicates. Please investigate."

Sam never provided any specifics of what the men talked about, where these men were located, or, for that matter, a description of the stray dog. Likewise, Sam never offered an opinion as to whether the duplicate replacements of his personal property were as nice as the originals, or perhaps better. In a way, Sam was a pleasant distraction to my day, and I began looking forward to his emails.

After I left the FBI spokesperson position, Sam continued to write. This went on for a number of years, so eventually the FBI finally determined where he resided, and a couple of agents paid him a visit. They reported back to me that Sam was harmless. "Crazy as a loon, but harmless."

Sam wrote to me daily, from his first email in 2004 until I retired in December 2015, at which time my FBI email address was discontinued. For all I know, he still may be writing.

Elvis

In a case involving possible public corruption by a police officer, I developed a source to whom I assigned the code name Elvis, because he bore a striking resemblance to Elvis Presley, albeit not the younger, more handsome Elvis.

In the case, it had been alleged that a police officer from one particular community was responding to after-hours burglaries at various businesses, and upon arrival, was helping himself to the store's items. *If this happened to be true, who would know?* Anything missing would be attributed to the burglar, and the store owner would include the items in any claim made to the insurance company. In turn, the officer who allegedly committed these thefts would then take the ill-gotten goods to a local pawnshop that didn't ask too many questions. I conducted some surveillance on the pawnshop.

Eventually, I observed a police car arrive and back in to the front door. I watched as the occupant of the vehicle popped open the trunk, removed his items and carried them inside.

This confirmed the information we had was likely good, but what I really needed was someone on the inside.

Enter Elvis. Elvis was a local mope. (Please see the definition of *mope* provided earlier in the "Catch Me if You Feel Like It" section of this book.) I'd encountered him during the investigation of another crime; he was a peripheral participant who wasn't of any particular importance, but someone who wasn't necessarily off the hook. I remembered he worked at this pawnshop, so I explained to him that he could help himself by helping me. He was all too willing to assist.

My plan was to have Elvis enter the pawnshop when the cop in question was going to be there. He'd be wired with a transmitting device that would allow me to hear what was going on inside the store and would capture every incriminating word. Other agents would be nearby. When we heard the information we needed, we'd swoop in and make an arrest on the spot.

Another agent and I met Elvis in a nearby parking lot and wired him up with the transmitter. From a distance, I watched as Elvis meandered up to the pawnshop, talking to me in a low voice and checking the equipment to make sure he could be heard: "Testing, testing. One. Two. Three. Four. Testing."

He opened the front door of the pawnshop and disappeared inside. We heard Elvis shout out his hellos to the store owner. Then everything went silent.

I fiddled with the dials and knobs on the equipment, but for all my efforts: nothing. I couldn't bring back Elvis's voice or the voices of the others to whom he was talking. *Was it some sort of technical problem?* Of all the times in the world for this to happen, it had to be at this crucial moment?

Almost an hour passed before Elvis finally emerged from the pawnshop and walked in the general direction of my car, which was concealed from the pawnshop's view. Upon arrival, Elvis climbed into my backseat. He was all smiles. "What a great conversation!" he said, barely able to conceal his excitement. "I got everything!"

Dejected, I broke the news to Elvis that something must have gone wrong with the equipment and we didn't hear anything. "Nothing was recorded," I said.

"Oh, don't worry," Elvis said. "You didn't hear anything because we weren't talking."

I was confused. I turned around in my seat and looked directly at him. "What do you mean you weren't talking?"

Elvis explained that as soon as he'd entered the pawnshop, he'd thought, *If the FBI is listening, maybe someone else might be listening, too.* So, to prevent anyone else from listening in, Elvis got this bright idea. He shushed everyone in the room to not say a word. He then acquired a piece of paper and wrote a note that indicated, "In case someone is listening, we shouldn't talk about the stolen items being pawned, but instead just pass notes back and forth."

I fought off the urge to yell at Elvis then and there, or suffer my own aneurysm. Doing my best to control my exasperation, I said, "Elvis, *we* were listening. The FBI. That was the whole point of you going inside. You wasted my time and everyone else's time and you brought me nothing."

Elvis smiled at me in the kind of way that let me know he wasn't stupid, and quite frankly, possibly even smarter than the FBI. "Don't worry," he said. "I got it covered. I kept all the scraps of paper I wrote on so you can show what was said."

But everything was in only Elvis's handwriting. Nothing from anyone else. I returned to the office and closed Elvis as my source.

Taco Hell

When developing rapport with a source, an agent should create an atmosphere where the source is so comfortable that a bond, almost a friendship, is formed. With this at work, the source will put forth their best effort. Even so, sometimes agents have to do things they wouldn't otherwise do.

One source lived with his ailing, elderly mother. I stopped by for a visit and found her hooked up to an oxygen tank, which she was dragging around the house while looking for cigarettes to continue her nonstop chain-smoking. The house was quite dirty and came with the same old excuse: they've been too busy to clean it up for some time.

I was offered a seat on the couch. Fearful that if I *did* sit down, I might stick to something that would prevent me from getting up without first removing my pants, I made up the excuse that I'd been sitting all day and preferred to stand.

The source was a potential informant for a significant drug trafficking investigation, so when he asked if I was hungry, I reminded myself that I definitely wanted to be in his good graces. I'd successfully avoided sitting down and had just begun to explain that I'd had a big lunch when the source interrupted and insisted I try one of his homemade tacos.

The adjoining kitchen was no cleaner than the rest of the house. A pan was on a nearby stove, and the source was about to cook with it. It looked as if it hadn't been washed since the Donner party had previously cooked one of their traveling partners in it.

"Mom," the source said. "Where's the meat to make tacos?"

While these fateful words worried me, it was his mother's response that shook me to the core: "On the kitchen counter where you left it yesterday."

He'd forgotten to put the beef back in the fridge. He'd left it out at room temperature for almost a full day. It was late spring and it must have been in the mid-70s inside their home. For a moment I wondered if because of the source's forgetfulness of having left uncooked meat on his kitchen counter for the past twenty-four hours, he would think twice about cooking and help me avoid having to dine in his petri dish of a house.

These thoughts were soon dashed from my mind; I heard him clanging the frying pan as he moved it onto the burner, and shortly thereafter, the sound of sizzling meat. "Cooking it will kill any germs," my source assured me. "It will make it just fine for eating." Apparently, my source believed being a drug dealer also gave him the expertise to qualify as both a health inspector and a chef. It was like watching a series on the Food Network in hell.

Without appearing rude, I began to look for a way to escape. My cellphone typically rang all the time, so why wasn't anyone calling me now and giving me an excuse to leave?

Within a few minutes, I was handed a plate of "fresh" tacos and told to make myself comfortable. I feigned having just received a text from my office. "There's an emergency and I need to go. Could I take the tacos with me?" I asked, thinking I'd throw them away and tell him later how good they were. The source agreed. I was home free.

Until … he met me at his front door. He had a couple of tacos wrapped up, but one was on a paper towel. "You have to try at least one before you go," he said.

Putting the needs of the FBI ahead of my need to avoid botulism, I bit into the taco. Without chewing, I swallowed a portion, along with my certifiable fear that I was also poisoning myself. I forced it down, then smiled. "Delicious," I managed to utter, with the permission of the Supreme Court that has ruled it's okay for law enforcement to lie to criminals, although such normally occurs during an undercover sting operation. The circumstances were warranted here as well, I decided.

I left my source's house, the to-go tacos in hand, jumped into my Bucar, and drove away. I made a few turns down various streets to put some distance between the source and myself and found a public trash can where I threw away the remaining tacos. Then, in an act of self-preservation, I shoved my fingers down my throat and forced myself to vomit up the half-eaten taco. It tasted no better on the way up than it did going down, but I figured I just saved a life: my own.

Before Hand Sanitizer Became Popular

I was helping a young agent who'd just started to develop a source. We drove together to the source's residence, where we were to meet with him and discuss how he could be of value to the FBI. Upon arrival, we approached the front door and knocked.

No answer. The source was expecting us at this time, so we knocked again. Waited. Then knocked again. And waited. We did this for some time.

Both the new agent and I eventually agreed we'd come back at another time. As we started toward our Bucar, we heard someone fumbling with the front door lock. We turned around.

The front door was open. There stood the agent's potential source, in the middle of zipping up his pants and fixing his belt. We walked up to him, and he offered his apologies for not answering the door immediately while extending his hand to greet me. A fraction of a second later, he explained he'd been in the middle of masturbating.

The new information greatly shortened the length of time I'd normally spend shaking hands. The source then turned to shake the hand of the young agent—who looked fear-stricken. I shot him a look that indicated, "I just shook this mope's hand, you are damn well going to do so also." Reluctantly, he did.

With the introductions out of the way, the future source invited us into his home. We sat in the living room and heard his sad tale about how he and his wife had recently lost their child. Regardless of the strange and bizarre greeting at the front door, one couldn't help but have empathy for a person who'd gone through such a terrible event. The source asked if we'd like to see photos of their child, to which we readily provided a positive response. I thought perhaps sharing a bit of his child's life might bring him some comfort. He left the room to fetch the photos and returned a moment later holding a small white box tied with a ribbon. He carefully removed the ribbon and lifted the lid of the box, revealing photographs.

He began to pass them out. I didn't know how young his child had been before his death, but I didn't expect what I saw. My best guess is that the child was only weeks old . . . pre-birth. That's right, the photographs clearly showed an early-stage miscarriage of a very young fetus.

"Excuse me," I promptly said. "Would you excuse the agent and me? We need to go to our car for just a moment." Once outside, I instructed the agent to get in the Bucar. "We're out of here."

This guy was crazy. I'd been exposed to bodily fluids and fetuses within the first ten minutes. I wasn't going to spend another second in his house waiting for something else to happen.

"Perhaps we should at least go back inside and say goodbye," the young agent said as we approached the car. I wasn't having any of it, saying, "If you don't get in the car now, I'll leave you here."

I produced from the glove box an industrial-size spray bottle of Purell hand sanitizer, which I applied copiously, in full view of the source, without the slightest regard as to whether or not he might be offended.

Despite the first meeting, we did end up returning several days later to meet again with the potential source after the other agent received a telephone call from him. Ironically, as crazy as this guy was, he actually did have some information to offer, and the new agent eventually opened him as a source. We assigned him the code name Spunky.

The Searches

When a case is put together, the hope is that it will lead to the lawful arrest of a criminal. In more cases than not, the FBI executes a search warrant on a home or business. The search warrant is approved in advance by a judge who concurs there's probable cause to believe agents will find evidence of the crime under investigation. The search warrant is usually served at 6 a.m., first thing in the morning. Courts have declared this to be a reasonable hour, plus it's easier to catch a potentially dangerous criminal off guard when waking them up by knocking on their door or ringing the doorbell. In the rare case when the criminal has a job, we want to get them before they leave the house.

If the search warrant is on a business, we'll go during normal business hours, but take steps to make sure we don't put the general public at risk. Regardless, no matter what the time of day, location, or circumstances, the one constant in serving a search warrant is that no criminal is ever happy to be greeted by the FBI.

One Angry Mother

I arrived at a home north of Phoenix with my squad. The property was in a rural area. Storage sheds and a couple of vehicles were spread out around the many acres surrounding the residence. I was the squad supervisor and would usually accompany my squad whenever they went out as a group, but I always tried to stay out of the way and let the case agent run the show. So, while other agents knocked on the front door to make an entrance, I stood on the perimeter of the land and watched the back of the house for any possible threats. Because I had a big piece of property to cover, I'd brought my Bureau-issued H&K 9mm submachine gun.

On my portable Bureau radio, I heard the agents had successfully entered the property and all was secure—albeit with an irate mother. Her son was the subject of the investigation, and she was angry that the FBI had intruded upon her home. When she then came crashing out the back door and marched in a swift pace directly toward me, I surmised one of the agents had probably told her to "take it up with the boss."

Certain I could handle whatever she intended to say or do, I asked her to slow down. She looked angry and didn't break her stride for even a second. I commanded her to stop a little more firmly, but by then she'd already covered over one hundred feet and was now within a few yards of having her nose in my face. *Did she actually want to hit me?*

I commanded her to stop a third time, but still she pressed forward. Whether by training or instinct, I swung my long gun into position and pointed it in her direction, which, due to her rapid march toward me, put the barrel just inches from her face. She stopped charging toward me.

But that was only because she fainted and fell to the ground. In the midst of her footrace toward me, she may not at first have seen me holding a weapon, but she clearly recognized it when she got close.

When she came to a few seconds later, she was fine. Oddly enough, she didn't seem to remember what happened or why she fainted. I slung my gun over my shoulder and rested it against my back. "Perhaps you skipped breakfast and that caused you to faint. Might I suggest we go back inside and get you a snack?"

Barking Up The Wrong House

As mentioned earlier, executing a search and arrest warrant is a regular part of an FBI agent's job. While all agents learn the necessary aspects of a proper warrant execution early in their careers, some agents pay better attention to the details than others.

We were preparing to execute search and arrest warrants on a couple that'd been downloading graphic pictures and videos of child pornography. The FBI investigation had shown that the female subject had also been engaged in various acts of bestiality with a large dog, the breed of which had yet to be determined. We try to keep FBI reports specific by identifying subjects by race and gender, so when we were done with the search, we thought our report should probably indicate Poodle or Pomeranian as well.

One of my problem-prone squad agents had been tasked with obtaining the search warrant for the specific apartment in which the subjects resided. This particular agent was very strong-willed and wouldn't take suggestions from others. When those suggestions came from me, her supervisor, they were actually orders, but she didn't let her firm belief that she knew better than others interfere with such mere details.

Without assistance or specific direction, and entirely on her own, the agent had surveilled the apartment for several days prior in an effort to establish who might be present within the residence. She saw little activity, and so the decision was made that, the very next morning, we'd hit the apartment with the search warrant in hand.

The apartment was not in the best of neighborhoods, so we brought a few extra agents, a few long guns, and a couple of machine guns, one of which I carried.

Upon arrival, we formed a line and approached the front door, where we would knock and announce ourselves. As we did this, neighbors from the apartment complex began to gather and watch. This happens on occasion. Before you know it, word spreads and crowds gather to watch the action and find out which one of their neighbors is in trouble with the law.

We banged on the door and announced "FBI" loudly for several minutes. We were looking for male and female accomplices in their early twenties, so I was more than a little surprised when two middle-aged males opened the door. About ten seconds into the verbal exchange with these two men, I became further concerned when it became readily apparent both were mentally challenged and had no idea what was going on. It was unlikely they understood what "FBI" meant, who *we* were, and quite possibly even who *they* were.

After a difficult five-minute conversation in which we tried to make ourselves understood—and likewise, understand what they were trying to say—it became clear: we were at the wrong apartment. Of all the apartment units in the complex, we'd happened upon a group home for mentally challenged individuals who were being transitioned into a more independent living situation.

The apartment complex was divided into sections, A and B. Both sections had the same unit numbers. Apparently, my strong-willed agent had spent her several days of prior surveillance, and taxpayer dollars, observing the wrong apartment. Fortunately, she had the correct address information in the search warrant. Because we hadn't stepped inside the wrong apartment, there was no harm, no foul, and because we hadn't actually arrested anyone, no one's civil rights had been violated.

In addition to the two mentally challenged apartment occupants I had to contend with, the crowd of anti-law enforcement onlookers was steadily growing restless. I decided it was time to depart before things became ugly, as this situation would likely lead to the media showing up, and then I'd have to explain what the FBI was doing there, or should not be doing there, in the first place.

In a moment of inspiration, I announced as loudly as possible for all to hear: "Okay, good practice drill, everyone! Get your gear and let's move to the actual location for the real thing!"

More quietly, I thanked the two apartment occupants whom we'd intruded upon for their time and assistance in helping train law enforcement in an effort to keep their community safe. I helped usher both individuals inside their home and shut the door behind them. Happily, neither man seemed in any way unnerved or even remotely fazed by the appearance of a dozen heavily armed law enforcement men and women outside their apartment door.

I never heard anything after this about having almost executed a search warrant on the wrong house. Maybe the men never told their group home supervisor. Maybe they did tell their story of what happened and it resulted in having their medications adjusted to prevent future hallucinations. Either way, it was a small price to pay to prevent embarrassing the Bureau.

Within a short time, we regrouped and found the correct apartment. We lined up at the front door and knocked to announce that the FBI had arrived and prepared for entry. It was Déjà vu all over again.

To my relief, the actual subjects, a man and a woman, appeared at the door this time. We handed them a copy of the search warrant and conducted a search of the apartment. During this time, the subjects were separated and interviewed by squad agents. I decided to sit in on the interview of the female subject, who'd apparently participated in the aforementioned bestiality photographs with a shepherd-type dog we later learned was named Cinnamon—which forever tainted my further use of that particular spice. Before me sat a pretty young lady who seemed completely normal, apart from the fact that I'd seen naked pictures of her engaging poor Cinnamon in compromising positions.

I'd barely sat down when the dog walked by. Cinnamon seemed happy to have new visitors to play with, and like the two men from the earlier apartment, appeared unfazed by our presence.

The interview had just begun, but I interrupted, unable to wait. "You gotta tell me," I said to the woman. "What's the deal with the pictures of you and the dog?" Tears began to well up in this young woman's eyes. Through quiet sobs, she explained they'd only posted a couple of explicit photographs of her and Cinnamon.

While she and her boyfriend were interviewed about their role in the crimes, the FBI searched her home. They would later be hauled off to jail, but at that moment the woman believed her biggest concern was having committed an offense where she had *posted* photographs on the internet of herself engaging in bestiality. She didn't seem to understand that bestiality itself was the issue. "All bestiality is illegal," I explained.

She said she didn't realize that and offered that the dog in no way had been harmed. "Just look at the pictures," she said. "Cinnamon seems happy." I told her there was no such thing as engaging in a consensual sex act with any animal, including a dog. "Woof means no."

He's Not Dead

At a similar search on another day at another apartment complex, my agents lined up single file to approach the door and make entry. On this particular day, I was about seventh in line, a good distance from the front of the line, when the first agent banged on the door.

"This is the FBI! We're here to execute a search warrant!"

If an occupant didn't open the door, the second agent in the line would wield a sledgehammer and take the door off its hinges. Which is precisely what was done.

However, as soon as the door crashed open, an odor wafted out that was so strong that it overpowered me all the way in the back of the line. I'd been in law enforcement long enough that I thought I knew exactly what the smell was and why nobody answered. There had to be a dead body inside.

We entered the small, cramped apartment and discovered the windows were shut and the heat was turned up. Had there been a dead body, we would've been lucky. We'd have called the coroner's office, and for the most part, the case would be over. Unfortunately, instead, we took turns holding our breath. Everywhere we looked and every time we inhaled, we caught wind of several years of dog urine and feces.

Apparently, our subject had never taken his dog outside and allowed the canine to do his business wherever he liked, probably because the criminal was too busy trading images of child pornography from his home computer. The odor was so intense that, after a few minutes, several of us began to wretch, so we decided to take turns searching the residence.

The subject of our investigation was found, very much alive, and arrested. The odor was the result of the conditions inside the apartment. With no likelihood he'd ever be released, we took the dog (with his permission—the subject, that is, although I'm sure the dog was equally agreeable) to a no-kill shelter so it could be placed in a new home. And, presumably, a yard.

Grandma Is Chicken

During the execution of another search warrant, I noted that the entire residence was filled with pictures and figurines of chickens: chicken ceramics on shelves, chicken paintings, and chicken clocks on walls. Everywhere I looked—chickens. It seemed an odd decor selection, but to each his own.

The subject of our investigation was a twenty-something man who lived in the house with his grandfather. My curiosity got the better of me and I couldn't resist, so I asked, "What's with all of the chickens?"

The grandfather explained that, after his wife passed away, he was convinced she'd come back as a reincarnated chicken. That explained why several hens roamed around their front and back yards, even though their house was located in an otherwise residential neighborhood. The grandson confirmed that he, too, shared the reincarnated chicken belief and the potpourri of poultry on display in their humble abode was their way of honoring her.

I decided not to mention that I'd had chicken for dinner the night before and that Grandma was delicious. Thereafter, on every occasion the squad would gather at some restaurant for lunch, someone would inevitably say, "I'm going to have the grandma."

One of the many chicken replicas placed in the subject's home as an homage to the grandmother whom he thought had returned as a reincarnated fowl.

Dial C For Confession

One of my agents investigated a case involving the theft of intellectual property. The subject possessed a legal DVD of a popular workout video in the form of a television infomercial, the kind you see advertised at all hours of the day and night. Because the series was expensive to purchase legally, the subject used his copy to make bootleg versions, which he then sold on the internet at a substantial discount.

Aside from the obvious loss of profits this theft caused the manufacturer of the video series, the consumers who purchased the bootleg copies received a far inferior-quality product, with grainy video and noticeably degraded audio reproduction. While the subject profited from his illegal business, the video company and the consumer were being ripped off.

Armed with the necessary probable cause, my agent obtained a search warrant, and we gathered outside the subject's residence one bright, early morning.

After the requisite knock (pounding) and announcement that the FBI had come calling, we waited for someone to answer the door. And waited. And waited. After a period of time with no response, we assumed no one was home. Or perhaps they hoped we would just go away, like an unwelcome religious proselytizer. Unfortunately for our subject, that's not how it works.

So, with no one to answer the door and no key to open it, I employed one of my most physically fit agents to activate the sledgehammer solution. She raised the sledgehammer as if she was going to ring the bell at a carnival. After just a few swings, she took the front door right off its hinges.

We made entry into the residence, cleared the house for safety, and quickly determined that no one was in fact home—which explained why no one answered the door, along with why there was no longer a door.

It had been our hope to interview the subject while he was at the residence, but the homeowner's absence had no bearing on our ability to conduct the search. The agents went about their business and looked through everything as they collected evidence, which included hundreds of illegally copied workout DVDs. During this time, the case agent called the subject's cellphone to speak with him and perhaps even have him return home and join our little gathering. He got the subject's voicemail and left a message in which he explained that he was with the FBI, and at that very moment, he was calling from the subject's very own living room.

The agent left his cell number and suggested the subject call back as soon as he could.

After years of dealing with various subjects, I'd not become immune to the fact that an encounter with the FBI could be disconcerting, especially when it involved special agents knocking your door off its hinges and rooting around your house, going through all your personal belongings in search of hidden evidence that may be used to convict you and send you to prison.

When people are under stress, they can become flustered and make mistakes. It's perfectly normal behavior, but in some cases, it can actually work in the FBI's favor. In this situation, after the subject received the case agent's message, he undoubtedly panicked. Instead of calling the agent back, as requested, he wisely decided to call his attorney instead.

In the stress of the moment, however, the subject dialed the case agent's cellphone number by mistake. We were all busy searching the house, the case agent included, so when his cellphone rang, he let it go to voicemail.

The outgoing voicemail message on the case agent's phone clearly stated, "Hi, you have reached FBI Special Agent..." Maybe because the subject wasn't a good listener and/or he was stressed, he didn't pay attention to the message. For whatever reason, the subject believed he had called his attorney. Operating under this mistaken belief, he proceeded to leave a lengthy message describing the illegal activity in which he was engaged, copying and selling the DVDs on the internet, which resulted in leading the FBI to his residence to conduct a search at that very moment. So much for needing the subject to volunteer a statement. He'd just provided a recorded confession, which included: "I hope the FBI does not look under the carpet in the hall closet, where I have a hidden safe."

Prior to leaving the residence, as a courtesy to the homeowner, we boarded up the door we'd knocked down—but not before we looked under the hall carpet!

Finding a mannequin placed in homes of subjects is not an unusual occurrence.

Some mannequins are more disturbing than others.

The Subjects

J ust as there are many kinds of FBI agents, there are many kinds of subjects. People who commit crimes come in all shapes and sizes and with all sorts of personalities. Some are hostile. Some are cooperative. Others are clever. Some display previously unseen levels of stupidity. But like snowflakes, each is unique in their own way.

Pulling A Rabbit From Her Hat

During the investigation of an alleged kidnapping of a child, we interviewed the father's girlfriend. She claimed the child was kidnapped right out of her vehicle while stopped at a traffic light. Her story fell apart in seconds. It became obvious to us that she was lying and had something to do with the missing child.

She said she was sitting at a stoplight for some time and no other cars were around. A car later pulled up alongside her car, and two male gangbangers pointed guns at her and demanded the child.

Her explanation that she'd sat at a stoplight for a long period of time with no other cars around was a strategic error on her part. We checked the intersection and found the traffic light had sensors that would automatically change the light to green if a car was waiting and there was no cross traffic. However, her real undoing was her description of the subject's vehicle. "It was a green Volkswagen Rabbit."

No self-respecting gangbanger would be caught dead driving a green Volkswagen Rabbit as their hooptie. It turned out she'd staged the whole thing in an attempt to extort ransom money from her boyfriend.

San Quentin

One of my sources, a big muscular guy, had been involved in gang activities and was street-tough. Whether he was out on the street or locked up in prison, he seemed to have little regard for his surroundings. To him, life was all the same: hanging out with his brother gang members or taking care of anyone who got in his way. I jointly operated this source with another agent.

One day, while our source was on parole, he was arrested by police for carrying a weapon. As this was a parole violation, he'd be headed back to prison, this time to San Quentin. This place was well-known to him from experience, and to me by the many early gangster movies as the place for serving hard time. He'd be locked up with a lot of people like himself, including those from other gangs. Before he was taken away, I asked him if he had any concern for his safety. "No," he said. "The first day, I'll just find someone bigger than me and beat him as a warning to everyone else."

"Not everyone will fare as well as you in prison," I said. He responded by telling me a story, common among his fellow inmates:

> One day, a mild-mannered white-collar criminal arrived for his first day at the men's correctional facility. He was ushered into the prison and brought

directly into the general population. This new prisoner was in fear for his life, and it showed. Seeing this, a very large and muscular inmate sauntered up to the new guy and put his arm around him. However, instead of threatening the fearful prisoner, he showed some compassion and said, "Don't worry. It ain't so bad in here. I will show you around, and you will make friends. Before you know it, you will be one of the guys."

The new prisoner visibly relaxed and settled down a bit.

At this point, his large inmate friend told him, "But here in prison, you are either the husband or the wife. You got to be one or the other. The good news is that in here, you get to pick which one you want to be."

The new prisoner thought, *I don't want to be either some inmate's husband or wife*, but he figured if he had to be in prison, he might as well make the best of it. "Well, if I have to choose, I guess I will be the husband."

"All right, then," said the large and looming inmate. "Get down on your knees and suck your wife's cock."

I later had the occasion to travel to San Quentin to meet with this source. I arrived at the prison, and it was just like the old movies. I stepped inside, and a giant twenty-foot steel gate clanked shut behind me. I continued to pass through a series of gates like this until I was locked in. No escape.

One of the guards, a really big fellow—bigger than my source—took me to a meeting room where I'd meet my source. This necessitated passing through an open prison yard on the way. It was there where I saw inmates in every direction, hanging out or exercising, every one of them looking menacing in their own way. The guard assured me we were fine, as none of the inmates would do anything because of the rifled guards in the towers surrounding the property. As we continued on our way through the yard, I heard a deep voice boom out, "Escort!"

Some background is in order.

San Quentin is where California carries out its executions. It's the home of death row and holds all the inmates in the state who have been convicted and sentenced to death. Years prior, when a death row inmate was escorted through the yard, the escorting guard would yell, "Dead man walking!"

This was done to let the other inmates know they needed to get out of the way and not to speak or make contact in any way with the death row inmate. The rules required that other inmates had to stop what they were doing, and actually turn to face in a different direction than the death row inmate. If you were on death row, special rules applied to you, such as who you were allowed to speak with—generally, prison personnel, visiting family members, or your attorney. The phrase *dead man walking* had become politically incorrect by that time, so now only one word was said: "Escort!"

Upon hearing this word, everyone in the yard immediately stopped what they were doing and faced away from the prisoner being marched out to death row. Everyone, that is, except my guard and me.

While we watched, the guard escorted his prisoner—who had both hands and feet shackled and a chain around his waist, forcing him to shuffle along in front of the escort guard because his feet were too restricted to walk at a normal gate. "Escort!" the escort guard declared occasionally as he moved his charge from one location to another.

The death row prisoner turned out to be a somewhat diminutive individual. Shackled and dwarfed by the much larger guard, he didn't look at all intimidating. As he passed my guard and me, I made eye contact with him. The prisoner smiled at me and gave a slight wave with his hands, which were secured to the chain at his waist.

After the prisoner had passed and was out of sight, my guard told me because no one is allowed to communicate with a death row inmate other than certain people, I am probably one of the few who'd been allowed to make eye contact with him in years, hence the smile and wave. "He looked harmless," I told the guard. "What did he do?"

"Oh," said the guard as we took the first step to continue on our way. "He ate someone."

Child Pornography Subjects

Believe it or not, there's a whole cadre of individuals out there who like to go online and look at images of child pornography. These graphic and disturbing images, in which children have been unwillingly victimized, can be emotionally difficult crimes for agents to work on, but extremely rewarding cases, as you are taking someone off the street who truly poses a very real threat to the community.

In working these cases as both an agent and a supervisor, it was common to find that someone who looked at such images for pleasure for years would eventually decide to act out their fantasies on a real child. Our goal was to arrest them before the predator could move on and hurt another child.

School Days

In my very first case as an FBI agent, I was assigned to a child pornography investigation. At the time, this was relatively new terrain for the FBI. Our involvement in these cases began just as home internet access was becoming more commonplace. At the time, I was using the Prodigy dial-up service to get on the internet, and AOL was just a twinkle in the computer user's eye.

My subject had been on the internet collecting numerous images of child pornography. Though he never did anything in person with a child, the mere viewing, downloading, and trading of child pornography images is a crime, as the mere viewing creates a demand for such materials, so I wrote a search warrant. The judge who reviewed the warrant was appropriately appalled at the subject's crime. At 6 a.m. the next morning, a bunch of my squad agents and I knocked on the subject's door to execute the search warrant.

On this occasion, as is frequently the case, we executed the search warrant with no plans that day to arrest the subject. If there was no concern over being a flight risk, it was better to use the evidence seized to put together an even stronger case prior to making the arrest. I seized his computer equipment as evidence, which in the short term would make it difficult for him to get online again. It was unlikely he'd flee, so there was no concern that he might become a fugitive.

Despite the fact that the house contained a few creepy items not listed to be seized in my warrant (and they added no evidentiary value to my case), such as the handcuffs permanently mounted to the headboard of his bed—I assumed those weren't there just in case he had to arrest someone in his sleep—the plan was to present my findings to a grand jury, obtain an arrest warrant, and return later to take the subject into custody.

On many occasions, subjects whose homes have been searched by the FBI won't be physically arrested, but will instead receive a letter stating they must turn themselves in. Sort of like the opposite of winning the Publishers Clearing House sweepstakes. The subject receives a letter announcing: "Hey, congratulations! You've been arrested by the FBI! Now please, with your legal counsel present if you so desire, turn yourself over to authorities at a particular time and place." Not exactly that, but you get the idea. In this case, however, because of the nature of the crime, my subject was to be picked up in person, just in case the receipt of such a letter might give him a change of heart and he'd consider fleeing.

I obtained my arrest warrant and it was time to pick up my subject, but I learned he wasn't home or at work. He was attending classes at the University of Michigan's Flint campus. In fact, he was in the middle of a final exam at that exact moment.

Normally in such a situation, I'd be inclined to wait until class was finished and arrest him afterward. However, because this was a final exam, the allowed time for the test was almost three hours. I needed to get my subject into custody and processed before it got too late in the day. He could appear before a judge the same day and possibly make bail to be released and go home. If I waited until after his exam, he'd spend a night in jail and see the judge in the morning. By arresting him sooner rather than later, I was actually doing him a favor. Plus, I had dinner plans. What to do?

After a half-second's hesitation, I opened the classroom door, walked into his exam, and was promptly greeted by the proctor's somewhat terse, "May I help you?" She was no doubt annoyed that I'd interrupted her exam, so I showed her my credentials and said, "FBI. I need two minutes of your class's time."

I turned to face the class. They stared back at me. "All right, class," I said. "May I have your attention? Everybody put your pencils down."

I addressed my subject by name and asked him to please stand up and come with me. I escorted him outside and into the hallway, where I handcuffed him. Just outside the door, with a grasp on my handcuffed subject, I ducked my head inside the classroom and told the class, "Okay. You may now pick up your pencils and resume your test. There will be extra credit for anyone in the essay portion of the exam who can correctly identify what just happened."

I later returned to the school with some follow-up business and was told, "Oh, don't worry, we've made arrangements for your subject to take the final exam." I explained I was not concerned about that, nor was my subject, as "whatever he's studying is probably going to be obsolete by the time he gets out of prison" in about ten years.

From that time on, I would work a lot of child pornography investigations over the years, initially as an agent and later as a supervisor, where I provided whatever support was necessary for my agents who worked the cases.

Every time we'd search one of these child pornography residences, it was a strange trip into a world that regular everyday people don't venture into. When the FBI executes a search warrant, we search every square inch of the house, because you never know where the subject may have hidden evidence. I've found photographs of child pornography saved to CDs hidden in the box springs of beds. I've found external hard drives loaded with child pornography images hidden in drop ceilings. You never know what you'll come across.

I've found penis-shaped pasta in the kitchen pantry and books with titles like *Tickle My Pickle* in the bookcase. The Holy Grail of all places to hide things? The subject's bedside table. Within those drawers lie sex toys for uses one wouldn't think were possible. Looking for a fake penis? Check the bedside table. Need a gallon of lubricant? It's in there as well.

I also found that people drawn to this type of crime gravitate toward professions that bring them close to children. While the vast majority of people in these professions are all good, decent, and dedicated individuals, there is a fractional percentage of the sordid kind. I've participated in the arrest of pediatricians, elementary school teachers, camp counselors, children's entertainers, and even a pediatric anesthesiologist. Also among those I've arrested were subjects who were equally dangerous, but not as bright.

Backfire

One day, as I worked in the FBI Flint office, a thirty-year-old man named Randy walked in. As the duty agent of the day, I had the good fortune to speak with Randy. He'd decided to visit the FBI because he claimed to have uncovered information about persons who'd been viewing child pornography, and he wanted to be a source for the Bureau. But Randy's story didn't make sense.

So, I conducted a little investigation and quickly determined that Randy himself was the person viewing and collecting the images of child pornography and had become paranoid that the police would find out and arrest him. I determined he'd concocted the idea of working as a source in the belief that he could claim anything he did in the past that was illegal was done on behalf of law enforcement, and he'd get the added benefit of continuing to view child pornography in the future.

One of my first clues was that Randy had married a woman half his age. That's right, he was thirty and she was fifteen when they married—with her parents' permission! Additionally, Randy was unusually close to his nephew, who was just a few years older than his child bride, although he was a legal adult. It seemed that Randy, in some dysfunctional family cottage industry, would have his wife and nephew scour the internet when he was too busy to do so himself and find pictures of child pornography for him. I eventually developed a case, arrested Randy, and delivered him to jail.

Shortly thereafter, a court hearing for the trial took place. Randy was allowed to take the stand, where he provided testimony in answer to his attorney's questions. Randy explained that he'd been framed and claimed he'd been an informant for me, and on behalf of the FBI, since April 1995. He'd been tasked as a source to help locate people online who traded child pornography. Randy explained he worked undercover, solely at my direction, and when I failed to put together any cases (due to my own incompetence), I framed Randy by arresting him and charging him with a crime.

It could have been a halfway decent defense, and it might have even convinced a jury by providing enough reasonable doubt that they would acquit Randy if it weren't for just one small detail: During the many months Randy alleged we'd met as agent and source, I wasn't even an FBI agent yet. In April 1995, I'd just arrived at the FBI Academy. I had four months of training ahead of me before I'd arrived at my first office.

The truth is, Randy had walked into the FBI office just three weeks prior to the completion of the case I'd built against him, resulting in his providing a full confession. Even after his confession, I allowed him to go home, knowing he had nowhere to run. I subsequently obtained an arrest warrant and then arrested him. His plan to blame others had backfired, and he'd ended up convicting himself. Randy's stories, lies, and arrest are interesting, but what I remember most about him occurred when he was initially in jail awaiting trial.

Randy really didn't like being in jail away from his computer, but he couldn't convince the judge to lower his bond enough for him to make bail. He decided if he could prove to the court that his life was in jeopardy while he was in jail, the judge might be more sympathetic.

Several weeks into his jail stay, after Randy had once again been denied a lower bond, I received a middle of the night telephone call from the jail where he was being held. According to the guard on duty, Randy had been taken to the infirmary, where he alleged that he'd been assaulted in his cell by cellmates who didn't like the fact that he was a pedophile. Initially, this all seemed plausible to me. One of the oddities of the jail hierarchy is that inmates don't take kindly to prisoners who abuse children.

I was about to ask for details about what had happened when the guard said Randy had in fact been sexually assaulted. *Yes, life behind bars could be rough*, I thought. But then the guard added, "And it appears to be self-inflicted."

In an attempt to gain sympathy from the judge, Randy had faked his sexual assault and blamed it on his cellmates in a convoluted attempt to justify why he shouldn't be in jail awaiting trial and be granted bond. Let your mind wander for a moment. Care to guess what Randy did to himself?

No matter what your guess is, you are incorrect. All these years later and I still have trouble comprehending his decision to do what he did. He'd found a paper clip and straightened it out. Claiming later that he was held down by cellmates, Randy falsely reported that they'd inserted this paper clip up and into the opening of his penis.

This would have been physically impossible. Visions of a frightened turtle come to mind. Even under general anesthesia, this would not be the easiest of procedures. I have trouble threading a needle, and the needle isn't fighting back or retracting itself. Before the call ended, the guard asked me, "What should I do?"

I thought for a moment, then suggested, "Throw a staple gun into his cell and let's see what happens next."

Pedophile Parenting

Shortly after the court cases involving Randy and his willing participant nephew were concluded, I sat at a little sidewalk cafe with my then-three-year-old son, when who should happen by but the mother of Randy's nephew?

She was upset. Understandably so—her child was going to prison. As so often happens, rather than recognize that her son was responsible for his own behavior and it was this that led him to prison, she was misguided and blamed me for what happened to him.

There I was, just trying to enjoy a quality father-and-son moment, but this woman was blaming me for the pain brought upon her family. I would normally be sympathetic to what she was going through, but confronting me in public in the presence of my young child was unnecessary. She then started to make a scene, and other people began to pay attention and listen.

I waited for a brief pause that finally came to her venting and took the opportunity to tell her, "As you can see, I'm the parent of a young child. I'm wondering if you have any parenting tips, so I can do the exact opposite."

That pretty much ended any further discussion.

Be A Doll And Help Me

As I mentioned earlier, when tracking subjects who deal in child pornography, it's not uncommon to find they've gravitated toward careers that bring them in close contact with children. So, it came as no surprise when the FBI learned a new subject had been identified who made his living for forty-plus years as a children's party magician.

The case agent obtained a search warrant, and we executed it upon the subject's home. We expected to find the usual disturbing pictures of children, along with all sorts of sex-related novelties. What we didn't expect was a house full of dolls.

Children's toy dolls of all shapes and sizes. In every room. On every chair. In every available space in the home, there was some type of little girl's doll. In the bathroom, a doll sat next to the sink. In the bedroom, numerous dolls sat on the dresser and stood in the closet. In the dining room, the dinner table came with four chairs: one, which was empty for the subject, and three others, occupied by dolls that were clearly there to keep him company. There appeared to be no adults in his life.

When he wasn't pursuing children, dolls were his only life companions. In addition to the dolls, a framed, full-color sketch naked rendition of Daphne and Velma from *Scooby Doo* sat on the bedside table next to a photo of his mother.

A search of the residence of an online child predator who lived alone revealed toy dolls situated throughout the house.

Hoarder House

On a search warrant, my squad and I arrived at a very nice upper-middle-class neighborhood with lovely homes throughout the block. In some places I've searched, you dread going inside the first time because you know from the general neighborhood that the homeowner won't impress anyone with their housekeeping skills. You also know the house will be a dirtier and more cluttered search. Based on the upscale and well-manicured community, I felt confident the day would be easy. I could not have been more wrong.

As usual, we politely announced our presence: "FBI! Search warrant! Open the door!" The occupants came outside. First the mom and dad, then their twenty-something son. We were fairly certain the son was the subject in this case, but when executing a search warrant, even though you've ordered everyone to come out of the

An abbreviated search was conducted of the home office rather than spend any unnecessary time in this hoarder subject's residence.

house, that doesn't mean all the occupants have cooperated. Anyone could still be inside, even an armed subject lying in wait. Once we were reasonably sure the building had been vacated, we would enter carefully and conduct a search to ensure no one remained behind. One step inside this residence and we knew this would not be a typical search.

This was a hoarder home. All those hoarder homes you've seen on reality TV don't even come close to what this was like. Garbage, chest-high, was piled throughout the entire house. A person could only make their way from room to room through the slim pathways carved through the densely packed stacks of trash and debris. Barely a few feet into the house, I saw all sorts of unbelievable things.

A partially eaten ham still on the bone sat on top of a pile in what was apparently the living room. Hypodermic needles were littered everywhere, including on the trail on which we walked. Occasionally, some small living creature would scurry through the mounds of trash. If anyone else was still in the house, they were either trapped and

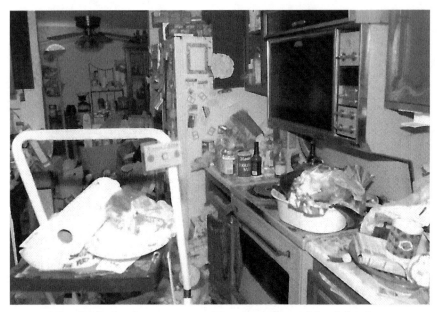

Very little food prep area remains in this subject's kitchen.

couldn't get out or they really wanted to stay, which was fine by me. Far be it for me to go in any farther or have to drag anyone else out.

I told my agents to back off and exit the way we came in. The house was clearly a fire risk to the entire community, although having it catch fire and burn to the ground would immediately increase overall property values. So, we called the fire department.

Upon their arrival, the firefighters took one look and immediately concluded, "Nothing is on fire. This is really a job for HAZMAT"— those specially trained to handle hazardous materials. So, we called in HAZMAT.

The brave souls of HAZMAT have seen all types of dangerous situations, like jet fuel leaking from an airplane or residential gas leaks that could explode at any moment. It takes a lot of guts to go to work every day and take on those dangers. Just one look inside the

My agents donned Tyvek suits that Hazmat was kind enough to offer after they declined to enter the subject's residence.

hoarder house and the leader of the team told me in no uncertain terms, "I'm not going in there."

It seemed as long as you were smart enough not to go inside, the house in question didn't pose an actual threat.

So, an executive decision was made by the HAZMAT leader to protect human life—namely, his own—and remain outside. In the event that I or my agents wanted to go back inside, he kindly offered the use of his team's white Tyvek suits, the sort of thing you've probably seen on shows like *CSI*.

In what would only become clear to me years later as another misguided attempt on my part to lead by example, another agent and I put on protective equipment and went inside. We opted to grab nothing more than the home computer and forgo the search altogether. The items in that house could have only been sifted through with the help of a bulldozer, so searching any further would have been in vain.

We got the computer and were ready to leave the property when Saul, one of my agents, informed me he must have dropped his government-issued cellphone when we first entered the residence.

Not wanting to be the subject of any Bureau discipline for having lost property paid for by the government, Saul suggested if a few of us went back inside and looked around, we might be able to find the cellphone.

I nixed that idea. I'd rather replace Saul's phone with money out of my own pocket than go back into that house and risk further contamination.

A few days later, the mother from the home called the FBI office. She asked for me by name. "I've found a cellphone," she said. I told her to keep it.

Does This Tarp Make Me Look Fat?

We executed a search warrant at another apartment complex. Prior to the investigation, we'd obtained a copy of the occupant subject's driver's license. We knew our subject was a big guy, probably tipping the scales at well over 350 pounds. My guess was he'd been skipping his workout regimen and sitting behind a computer screen all day looking at child pornography. Agents knocked. Made the announcement.

The subject shouted through the door that he was home but couldn't immediately come outside. *What? The heck you can't. The FBI just told you to come outside with your hands up.*

I was stacked at the door with the other agents. Our guns were pointed in the direction of the subject. We were prepared to enter the apartment, if necessary. The agent argued with the subject: "No excuses. You are to exit the apartment immediately with your hands in the air." She was directly in front of me when she gave the command: "Come out! Come out!"

To everyone's surprise—and frankly, disgust—the 350-plus-pound subject emerged—stark naked. This is one of those certain visions you can never erase from the mind's eye. My agent continued to motion at him with her hand and yell, "Come out! Come out!"

I was so grossed out by the sight of this naked, obese hairy fellow that I started yelling, "Go back! Go back!" Regardless of my wishes, the subject continued to comply with my agent and remained outside his premises. Eventually, someone found one of those big blue plastic pool tarps and wrapped him in it, sparing the neighborhood and what was left of my psychological well-being.

His Kind Of Agent

The arrest involved a typical child pornography subject: heavyset, never went out in the sunlight, and sat behind the computer all day. That sort of guy. He lived in a small apartment, which most of the squad was busy searching for evidence. The case agent and I escorted the subject outside and located a nearby table, where we hoped casual conversation would lead to a confession.

"You're not under arrest," we told him. "This is not a custodial interview." That means he wasn't deprived of freedom of movement. He could get up and leave if he wanted. We made it crystal clear: "You can answer questions or not answer. It's up to you."

We were executing a search warrant, so we already had plenty of evidence to make a case, but any other evidence we found, or a confession, would be the icing on the cake. A confession generally leads to a plea bargain agreement, meaning no one wastes a lot of time or taxpayer money going to court.

The guy readily admitted what he'd been doing and said he liked communicating with kids, specifically young girls. He explained he was not really attracted to people his own age. The case agent was a thirty-something female, petite, who looked young for her age, in a 21 Jump Street sort of way. She inquired, "Are you attracted to adults at all?"

"Well, I might be," the subject replied. "But not necessarily."

"What kind of adults would you be attracted to?"

"Well," the subject said honestly, "I'm attracted to you."

The case agent looked pale from revulsion, but I had nothing to say as I was too busy trying not to laugh and barely kept myself from falling out of my chair.

Although this van turned out to be not associated to the aforementioned cases, the license plate gave rise to what we in law enforcement call "a clue".

The Arrests

From the moment a new agent enters the FBI Academy, the focus is about making an arrest. Once agents graduate and report to their first office, the pressure is on to prove their mettle in the field by putting a case together, getting a judge to approve an arrest warrant, and then slapping the handcuffs on their subject.

From the outside, it all probably seemed very *Law and Order*-like—it was serious work, with serious criminals pursued by serious FBI agents. Sometimes it actually happened that way, but like everything else in law enforcement, there were unusual moments that lightened the mood.

Getting A Confession

It was not uncommon to arrest multiple subjects at the same time. When I was with the police, we would often bring in two or three subjects caught during break-ins or driving a stolen car. Arresting someone in the act was one thing; getting a confession was another story. Even if you've caught someone in the middle of committing a crime, they could always claim they were just wandering by and found the place broken into before the police arrived and say, "We were just about to call the police."

In situations where criminals were not being cooperative, it behooved me to have them gang up on one another. There is no honor among thieves. Once a member of the group believed another member might sell him out, it was off to the races to see who would confess first.

One day, three young men, dressed alike in the same gang colors, were caught breaking into vehicles. They all refused to talk, so it was hard to determine who was the ringleader or if still others might be involved. At the police station, we placed each of them in separate holding cells and let them wait a while. After about twenty minutes, I removed one of the subjects from his cell and explained it had been such a busy night, I couldn't even remember who I'd brought him in with. They were all dressed alike, so I found this funny, but the subject did not seem to make that connection.

I walked my subject to the second prisoner's cell and opened the door. I pointed at his fellow criminal seated on the bench and asked, "Is that him?"

To which the first prisoner replied, "Yeah, that's him."

I repeated this same method with the third prisoner, then returned my arrestee to his cell. Of course, I thanked him for his assistance in helping me identify with whom he had been arrested.

I then visited prisoner number two and number three individually. "Well," I said. "You heard your friend. He gave you up—the break-ins were your idea. Do you want to make a statement or just take the fall all by yourself?"

Inevitably, number two and number three couldn't wait to talk. Nor could prisoner number one, especially once I'd informed him of what his colleagues had said about him.

Alternatively, sometimes subjects would implicate themselves. While a police officer I was out on patrol one night when I pulled over a car for a moving violation. The driver claimed to have forgotten their driver's license, but when I asked, they provided a name and stated their date of birth was June 31, 1970.

"Step out of the car please and put your hands behind your back."

"But what did I do officer?"

"I don't know yet, but there are only thirty days in June so I know you did something." Sure enough they had provided a false name and had outstanding warrants.

Say What?

I arrested a deaf bank robber not far from the downtown San Diego bank he had robbed only minutes before. I was placing my unsuccessful robber in the back seat of my Bucar, which was parked in front of the bank, when a somewhat arrogant criminal defense attorney whom I'd had the misfortune of encountering previously in my work just happened to wander by.

This was the sort of attorney who'd cross-examine me on the witness stand and try to convince the jury I was a liar and his client was just an honest person framed by the government. As if I had nothing better to do than accuse innocent people of crimes.

For the record, I had better things to do. Like investigate actual guilty criminals like the one I now had in the back seat of my Bucar. Nevertheless, defense attorneys have their job to do and I understood that.

Everyone has their constitutional right to a proper defense, no matter how guilty they may be. But please understand that law enforcement does not give rides in the back of their cars for no reason at all. Generally, you have to have done something bad to find yourself handcuffed in the backseat of a police car.

This was an attorney whose mission in life was to protect folks from people like me while I was trying to protect everyone else from people like his clients. That's the way the system works. I understood his job as an attorney was just part of the process. After all, I was a recovering attorney myself. I'd completed most of my steps in the Former Attorney Recovery Program. Step number seven: "God will never give us as many billable hours as we need to make the law firm's senior partners happy."

As I placed my deaf bank robber in the backseat, my legal adversary recognized me—and clearly noticed I'd taken someone into custody. Without hesitation, he changed direction, and literally pushed past me so he could speak directly to the bank robber seated in the car. Even though a defense attorney, he'd apparently decided to forgo a billable hour (likely his first time ever doing such a thing) and instead chose to dispense some free legal advice to my prisoner. He made it obvious he did this in an effort to spite me by circumventing my efforts, rather than provide any real assistance to the robber. However, before he got started and could say a word to the bank robber, I told the attorney: "Look, this guy is a hard case and could use all the help he can get. I know we have had our differences, but if you would be good enough to talk with him and give him the benefit of your legal genius, I won't stand in your way."

With that, the attorney's face lit up. He leaned into the open rear door of the Bucar and started saying all sorts of things to my deaf villain, like, "Don't say a word to this FBI agent." He regaled the bank robber with all sorts of legal advice from his years of experience. He was on a roll and must have gone on for ten or fifteen minutes before he'd exhausted dispensing all his knowledge. All the while, the deaf bank robber just looked at him with a blank stare and occasionally nodded his head, not that he actually heard anything.

I think the bank robber was trying to pacify the attorney so as not to appear rude. For all the deaf robber knew, the attorney was another agent. I think perhaps the robber wished to appear cooperative. Alternatively, maybe the bank robber assumed he was being read a very long version of his Miranda rights.

After the defense attorney completed his egotistical soliloquy, he turned to face me and proceeded to tell me he might've misjudged me, and I was a class act for allowing him to speak uninterrupted with the prisoner. He said other FBI agents could learn from this experience, recognizing that criminal defense attorneys and law enforcement could work together to help such an unfortunate person as this fellow in the back of my Bucar, perhaps even allowing the bank robber to go free.

"No problem," I said to my legal adversary. "I just hope that in some way I have made a difference today. I know that personally, you spending so much of your valuable time speaking to my prisoner has made a real difference for me."

Miss Opportunity

After I got the deaf bank robber secured in the back of my car, none of the other agents at the crime scene wanted to assist with the work that remained to process him. The arrest is the fun part; afterward, comes the chore of paperwork. This included interviewing the subject and taking his statement. Throw in the fact that this guy was deaf—which meant the interview would probably take hours longer than usual—and suddenly all the agents had other obligations. No one wanted to be involved in the aftermath.

I should mention that, during this time, I happened to be assigned to a squad that consisted of an unusually large collection of strong egos. This particular squad handled the reactive crimes: bank robberies, kidnappings, extortions, and the like. After spending so much time in this kind of work, some of the agents developed inflated egos and thought they were more important than other agents because they were actually out in the field "fighting crime." But this was totally untrue.

None of us on the squad were *actually* "fighting crime"; it was more like we just weren't getting along well with crime. Oh, there was plenty of crime to fight with, but there was always so much of it that there was little time to take off the gloves and duke it out. Instead of having an all-out schoolyard fight with crime, it was more akin to a junior high school locker room gossip against crime. We'd talk about what we'd responded to and what we saw, but before much could be done, we were off to the next robbery.

Don't get me wrong—like all agents in the FBI, these egocentric individuals were well-educated and functioned properly enough as FBI agents. It's just that each of them had quirky personalities mixed with their inflated egos, which made it less than desirable to spend extended periods of time in their presence.

For example, there was an extremely arrogant male agent who openly questioned the integrity of others while secretly having an affair with someone's wife.

There was also the extremely large, angry female who frequently criticized the actions of others, especially other women, in what others speculated was an attempt to conceal her own insecurities.

Another male agent looked so youthful that he constantly sought to prove his manhood. People regularly questioned if he was really an agent because he looked like he belonged in high school. He looked more like he should be on a bike delivering your newspaper, not investigating federal crimes. Occasionally, I even questioned him as to whether he had a note from his mother allowing him to play with the FBI.

Of course, constantly being challenged on his status as an FBI agent caused him to suffer from insecurities, thereby creating the need to constantly prove his manliness. In his eyes, if you were an agent who didn't engage in dangerous pursuits (SWAT, pursuing fugitives, etc.), you couldn't possibly be a real agent. As long as he continued to deliver my newspaper on time, that was fine with me.

The agents were still good at their jobs, but because of their negative and difficult personalities, I nicknamed the squad the Island of Misfit Toys, which probably made me Hermey the dentist.

None of these particular squad mates were about to offer their assistance with the deaf bank robber, especially when my arrestee was going to be a hassle and there was manly work to be done, even for the one on the squad who was a woman. Yet, I still had to attend to my bank robber.

Dealing with bank robberies post-arrest could be time-consuming in ways beyond conducting the interview and writing up a report. An arrest would pull an agent away from other pending responsibilities and certainly away from working on other pressing cases. Throw in the fact that my robber couldn't hear a single word and I was looking at three times longer than usual to get all the necessary work completed.

Fortunately, the Bureau contracted with sign language interpreters for just such occasions. Guess who turned out to be the sign language interpreter who showed up to assist me? Miss California from the Miss America pageant! Sign language interpretation was the talent and skill she used in her pageant competition, and here she was to help me, and the FBI.

When word got out that Miss California had arrived, Team Misfits was suddenly very interested in participating with my deaf bank robber's post-arrest. By that point, however, I had things well under control. I politely declined their offers of assistance. Besides, for one of them, it was collection day on his paper route.

Hence, while the rest of the squad spent the day dealing with regular crimes committed by regular criminals—the kind without hearing disabilities, just regular everyday communicable diseases—I got to spend my day interviewing the subject with Miss California.

As usual for me when interviewing a subject, I was pleasant toward my deaf bank robber. Treat people with respect and most will respond positively, even if that means confessing to a crime they committed that would send them away for many years. Even though I'd facilitated the loss of their freedom, many a subject has actually shaken my hand and thanked me for treating them so well on their way to jail. In many ways, interviewing a subject for the first time can be like a first date.

"So, I grew up in New Jersey and I have a brother and two sisters," I'd say. "But enough about me. Let's talk about you. So, where did you hide the money?"

When you're interrogating someone who is hearing impaired, you have to be extra patient. During one point, I asked the bank robber a complicated question, and Miss California signed with her hands for what seemed about thirty seconds. The guy moved his hands around in response for about the same amount of time.

Miss California turned to me. "He said 'no.'"

I looked blankly at her. "You're telling me it took all that just for him to say no?" Through the glimmering lips of Miss California, my deaf bank robber told me no, and also that he was hungry. Speaking of food, I was already thinking of asking Miss California to join me for an early dinner when were finished.

I understood the interpretation the first time, but as I recall, I asked him to repeat himself so I could continue to stare into the eyes of Miss California. I did that multiple times throughout the interview, which meant it was going to take us much more than just three times the normal length of time for a prisoner interview. What the heck. She was being paid by the hour, and I was by now clearly very smitten—with Miss California, not the bank robber—although I'm sure he also possessed some very fine qualities. However, I was in the presence of a beauty queen and planned on enjoying every possible moment of the experience.

With the hunger of my deaf arrestee verbally and visually expressed through the pouty lips and come-hither eyes of Miss California, I tracked down one of the cheerful FBI support employees who always baked cookies and brought them into work (a.k.a. Susie Sunshine, as everyone in the office called her). Ms. Sunshine informed me she'd gladly share a few cookies with me so I could feed my prisoner.

My deaf robber thanked me for being so considerate, and for the great-tasting cookies. So, in exchange for my hospitality, he decided to repay my kindness by telling me all about a couple of murders he committed. Could that day have been any better?

When Miss California agreed to join me for a meal, it absolutely did get better! I was married, so it was all very innocent, but I was definitely enamored. Had I known my wife would divorce me a decade later, I might have asked Miss California at that moment if she'd be willing to wait for me ... and my ex's future divorce attorney.

Stop And Smell The Roses

Arrests could be time-consuming, all-encompassing events. Unless it was an arrest made during the commission of a felony or serious misdemeanor, FBI policy required that agents first prepare a written operations (ops) plan, detailing which agent will do what, where the closest hospital is located (should someone be shot or injured), and all other sorts of details. This was mandated based on experience to ensure all arrests were carried out in the safest manner possible. Hence, this created even more (albeit important) work for the already overtaxed agent. However, this still didn't mean an agent shouldn't take a moment to enjoy the simple pleasures of life.

While assigned to Detroit, I was asked to assist with the arrest of a subject who—motivated by greed to collect on a large life insurance policy—faked his own death. He made it look as if he'd fallen off his boat and drowned, although the body was obviously never recovered. His family eventually collected the money and shared a large portion of the proceeds with the subject, who remained in seclusion. Somehow, however, years later a determination was made that the subject was actually alive. Good detective work located him living way up north, just blocks from Lake Michigan.

Early one morning, another agent, a couple of local officers, and I visited the home where the subject had been residing and took him into custody. It was all very uneventful. He seemed relieved to be arrested and no longer on the run. We then had about a four-hour car drive back to Detroit ahead of us. I thought, *I've never seen Lake Michigan. And it is so close by.*

I suggested to the other agent and the subject that we make a quick pit stop to take a look. After all, what's a few extra minutes in a four-hour car ride? The subject was more than agreeable; although he was glad to no longer be on the run, he was in no actual rush to go to jail.

I drove the three of us to Lake Michigan, where we got out of the car to take a closer look—with the subject cuffed behind his back. To record our special moment together, I retrieved a camera from the trunk of the Bucar and asked a person passing by to take a picture of the three of us. There's always time to stop and smell the roses—especially when you're going to prison and won't be seeing any for a few years.

You Talking To Me?

There once was a very nice female agent, a really pleasant lady who probably did not have the right personality for law enforcement. She was very smart, but seemed more akin to someone who worked every day helping people, not arresting them. One day, she was participating with other agents in the apprehension of a fugitive, a tough guy living with his tough girlfriend. Prior to the arrest, agents were warned to be careful, as both persons were considered armed and dangerous. They were to be treated as such until everybody was in handcuffs and secure.

At the house where the fugitive was holed up, the female agent bravely hit the front door and entered the home with several others, including some local law enforcement officers.

Startled by the sudden entrance, the fugitive and his girlfriend, who'd both been lounging on the couch, jumped to their feet at the sound. Without being asked, the fugitive, who knew the routine, got down on his knees and put his hands on top of his head.

In front of the pack of law enforcement officers was the female agent who faced the two subjects and pointed her gun at them. As the fugitive knelt, his girlfriend stood by his side. That's when a gruff cop who'd been around the streets awhile spoke up and yelled at the subject's girlfriend, "Get down on your knees, bitch!"

Thinking she might be in the way and the cop was speaking to her, the female agent complied and knelt. The cop who ordered the command responded with, "Not you! Her!" and pointed at the fugitive's girlfriend.

The now much-embarrassed female agent got back on her feet, and everyone laughed so hard that all assemblance of composure was lost, including that of the subject and his girlfriend.

Later, the very nice female agent left the FBI and went into the medical profession. I heard she was doing very well and was working under conditions that would never lead her to mistakenly believe a colleague would call her by any other name than doctor.

Hide-And-Seek Gunplay

While being apprehended by several agents, a bank robbery subject resisted arrest, and a minor wrestling match ensued. Until, that is, a gun fell to the ground and an agent yelled, "He's got a gun!" In an attempt to control the subject, he was forced to the ground, but landed on top of the weapon. A full-on fight broke out with punches thrown by everyone, but the subject was outnumbered. After a short time, the agents gained the upper hand, got control of the subject, and handcuffed him.

At this point, the gun was secured from underneath the subject. Only then did one of the agents realize the gun was his. It must have fallen out of his holster during the initial scuffle; the robbery subject had been unarmed.

Finally, not every subject will attempt to avoid being taken into custody. Under the right circumstances, they are more than happy to give themselves up.

During the middle of winter in Flint, Michigan, a robber decided to hold up a bank using a unique escape plan. He did not have an accomplice getaway driver or even a getaway car, for that matter. Instead, he brought a snorkel and flippers with him to the bank.

It seemed the robber selected a bank on the actual banks of the Flint River. After robbing the bank, his escape plan involved fleeing on foot to the river, putting on his mask and snorkel, and then making a getaway where no police cars could follow.

Maybe he was hard up and needed the money right away or maybe he did not own an outdoor thermometer, but in either case the bank robber did not get very far. As the temperature was below freezing and the only reason the river was not frozen was because the water was moving, once in the water the robber quickly began to suffer hypothermia. Police found him downstream a few minutes after departing the bank, where he profusely thanked officers for arresting him.

As one of my instructors from the police academy days was fond of saying, "Sometimes we only catch the stupid ones."

The attention to detail is always the mark of a good bank robber.

Epilogue

Within days of retiring from the FBI, the Bureau contacted me and hired me back as an outside consultant, leveraging my twenty years of FBI knowledge to work on some special projects.

Being asked to return to the FBI afforded me greater freedom to come and go as I pleased and again granted me access to the secure FBI building. Once or twice a week, I'd stop by the office to send work-related emails (on a secure computer) or speak with someone in another office (on a secure telephone line).

In the Phoenix building where I had previously been the ASAC, the FBI arranged a nice office for me. However, I didn't want to be a distraction in any way to the person who replaced me, so I requested a desk in the out-of-the-way supply room. This way, I could come and go without being seen by my former employees. It also gave me unlimited access to office supplies, many of which are still being put to good use in my current private speaking and consulting business.

Since then, I've moved beyond the supply room. I've provided consulting services to a number of significant clients, the professional sports world, Hollywood movie projects, and many large corporations. I've even returned to the Vatican to assist as needed.

I've also spent quite a bit of time traveling the country, speaking to corporate America in conferences on a variety of law enforcement topics such as terrorism, cybersecurity, active shooters, and leadership. I've also appeared regularly on the national news as a law enforcement contributor and have attempted to bring clarity to confusing topics.

I had a great career in the FBI, and I'm enjoying myself just as much in my work today. I like to think that in some small way I made a difference while I was a special agent and I'm continuing to make a difference now, yet still finding humor in everything I do.

In the end, maybe that's the secret to happiness. No matter what you do or where you work, in our own way, we should each try to make a difference to better the lives of others, whether through our work or by sharing a laugh. Preferably both.

By the way, if you need any office supplies, I can totally hook you up.

Acknowledgments

I first decided I wanted to be an FBI agent after attending a ninth-grade career day event at Memorial Junior High School in Fair Lawn, New Jersey. One of my teachers volunteered her husband, a special agent assigned to the FBI's New York Division, to spend the day talking with students. From that moment forward, I knew the FBI was the career for me, leading me to take steps to become qualified to apply.

One of those steps was gaining real-world law enforcement experience as an officer with the San Diego Police Department. During my initial thirty-two weeks of academy training, I met Chula Vista police recruit David Eisenberg who, to this day, remains one of my closest and most important friends. David and I survived the academy by sharing the same sense of humor, seeing the odd and ironic in everyday situations that most people ignored. Already a PhD when he entered the academy, David's cerebral approach to problem solving was always with a touch of humor. This encouraged me to develop my own style in conducting police work and allowed me to be myself without feeling I had to pretend to be the stereotypical image of what others thought law officers were thought to be.

My police academy training officer was Boyd Long, who eventually rose to become the department's assistant chief, and who tolerated all of our comments while his quiet demeanor tried to hide his grin, thereby encouraging such behavior.

My training officer in the field was Jerrilove Crocket (yes, that is her real name). She taught me what it was like to work the streets. That is, when she didn't have me chasing stray kittens at 2:00 a.m., which she was forever bringing home to foster. I also partnered for a while with Steven Douglas, who is literally one of the smartest people I have ever met. He can speak intelligently on any subject and would have made a great doctor, lawyer, or mad scientist had he not gone into law enforcement. Both Jerrilove and Steve motivated me to pursue the FBI.

Captain Lee Vaughn recognized a quality in me and regularly offered words of support. When he learned I'd been offered the opportunity to leave the department to pursue a career in the FBI, he encouraged me. During lineup on my last day with the department, Captain Vaughn wished me well with the admonishment, "The two most overrated things in the world are home cooking and the FBI." He was only correct about one of the two.

In the FBI Academy, classmate Jeff Eberle could impersonate anyone, including (much to their chagrin) all of our instructors. During our training, between getting knocked down in boxing and being pepper-sprayed in the face, Jeff's impersonations made the academy a fun experience. Ancil "Coach" Sparks was one of those instructors. He taught us never to take anyone we met for granted, imparting the lesson that "everybody is a potential somebody." His advice helped me build rapport with people I might have overlooked.

After graduating from the academy, my FBI training agent in Flint, Michigan, was Gary Reinecke. He taught me about working in the field, including ways to survive on a paltry government salary. He frequently quoted his personal mantra: "If it's free, it's for me."

The man who recruited me into the FBI, Larry Campbell, tolerated years of my telephone calls as I reminded him about my interest in becoming a special agent while waiting to be hired. He and his wife, Mary, became close friends and are the godparents of my daughter.

I would be remiss if I did not mention the man who gave me my first job out of college, Warren Neumann, a former police detective-sergeant who also did a few things on the side for another three-lettered government agency. Warren is the godfather of my son.

During my time in the FBI, I encountered many agents with a healthy sense of humor, as the FBI purposely recruits those who have outgoing personalities. The funniest were usually also the smartest, the likes of which included Tom Petrowski, FBI agent and legal counsel extraordinaire. In the wisdom of the FBI, 6-foot-2-inch Tom, broad-shouldered and even whiter than I am, was assigned with me to conduct surveillance on an African-American street gang, for which the Bureau issued us a large white Ford Crown Victoria police car—which made us stand out in the neighborhood even more than we already did.

Likewise, Adam Lee and Bob Foley were two agents with whom I worked who rose in the ranks to become special agents in charge of their own divisions. We worked cases together and shared plenty of laughs when sometimes there was little in the world that was funny. The three of us all share the same sense of humor and they provided great input of stories that have been included in the book.

One of the best bosses I ever had was Assistant Director Jana Monroe, who also happens to be the real-life inspiration for Jodie Foster's character in *The Silence of the Lambs*. Many of the stories in this book come from my time working for Jana, who, like me, embraced the humor found in our work.

The night before Thanksgiving, I found myself sitting in Jana's office at FBI headquarters long after everyone had left for the day. So comfortable was our relationship that, while she sat at her desk and we chatted, I slouched in a chair with one foot propped on the corner of her desk. In walked then-FBI Director Robert Mueller.

Long before he became special counsel and investigator of presidents, Director Mueller was an imposing figure who demanded absolute professionalism. Knowing I had just been caught lounging about, I jumped immediately to my feet. Somewhat instinctually (some might say cowardly), I moved to stand behind the chair in which I had been sitting.

Director Mueller greeted Jana and wished her a happy Thanksgiving. He then turned to me, held out his hand, and introduced himself. "Hi, I'm Bob Mueller."

To which I blurted out, "Of course you are."

The director gave me an odd look, pulled his hand back, and left the room without saying another word. Lesson learned: you never get a second chance to make a first impression.

Excellence apparently runs in the marital family, as Jana's husband, Dale Monroe, was a Marine officer helicopter pilot and retired special agent who was a member of the FBI's elite hostage rescue team. The respect I have for Jana and Dale is immeasurable, and both have been friends, supporters and mentors to me throughout my career and beyond.

I worked for four different FBI Directors during my career and would like to especially acknowledge former FBI Director Louie Freeh. I had the occasion to work briefly for Director Freeh and found him to be one of the most gracious leaders I have ever encountered. He never forgot his roots as an FBI special agent, and he treated everyone he encountered with respect.

James Turgal was another of my bosses who tolerated my sense of humor. During a Phoenix Division executive meeting, he announced that one of the office supervisors had suddenly gone blind in one eye, to which I stated aloud, "That's what he gets for masturbating so often." (Lack of empathy aside, the supervisor did get his eyesight back.)

Likewise, former Phoenix personnel with whom I shared laughs and friendship were SAC Doug Price, ASAC Andy Black, and especially ASAC Cary Gleicher (who was kind enough to transfer from Phoenix so I could be promoted as his replacement). Also, some of my exceptional and good humored agents included Julie Halftery, Michelle Pickens, Mike Boady, Paul Schaaf, Michael McAndrews, Travis Hatch, and Supervisor Martin Hellmer.

There are too many others throughout my law enforcement career to mention, including those colleagues we lost along the way when they made the ultimate sacrifice. I am sure my former police academy mate, running partner, and friend, Maria Larsen, is still on patrol in heaven when she's not putting aside her law enforcement duties to rescue stray dogs.

Finally, as much as anyone, I would like to acknowledge my children: my son, Garrett, and my daughter, Samantha. While the FBI caused me to miss moments in their lives, both of my kids were supportive of my career. Work pulled me away from birthdays, ballgames, holidays, and special events, and even Sam's eighth-grade graduation (although I have always been there to meet her boyfriends and show them my gun collection). Thank you both for putting up with me while being the most wonderful children a father could ever hope to have.

The kids are making their own contributions to the world. Garrett served as a US Army infantry soldier and spent a year in Afghanistan and is now a writer. Samantha studied psychology and is working to help others who are less fortunate. Both now strive to make the world a better place, each in their own way. A good legacy for me to leave indeed.

—John Iannarelli
April 2021

About The Author

John Iannarelli (a.k.a. "FBI John") served for more than 20 years as an FBI Special Agent and was also the Bureau's national spokesperson. His investigative work included the Oklahoma City Bombing, the 9/11 attack, the shooting of Congresswoman Gabrielle Giffords, the Sony hack, numerous bank robberies, kidnappings, and other assorted crimes. He is the recipient of the FBI Director's Distinguished Service Award, as well as an Honorary Doctorate of Computer Science.

John is a former San Diego Police Officer and graduate of the University of San Diego School of Law, having also completed international studies at Oxford, England. In addition to being a national news on-air consultant, he is an attorney, the author of five books and a highly sought-after keynote speaker. John is a Certified Special Professional (CSP®) by the National Speakers Association. He has presented to numerous Fortune 500 companies, domestic and international audiences, the United Nations, and the Vatican, where he has personally met on several occasions with Pope Francis.

You can learn about John's services by visiting his website FBIJohn.com and follow him on Twitter @FBIjohn.

Other Books By John G. Iannarelli

The Eighty Thieves: American P.O.W.s in World War II Japan (1991, with Anthony Iannarelli)

WTF: Why Teens Fail—What To Fix (2012)

Information Governance and Security: Protecting and Managing Your Company's Proprietary Information (2014, with Michael O'Shaughnessy)

How To Spot a Terrorist Before It's Too Late! (2016)

Made in the USA
Columbia, SC
29 August 2024

40751962R00124